#CONFIDENCE

#CONFIDENCE

How to build the confidence to succeed at love, life, work and play.

Su Birch

Published by Yes!Press,
an imprint of Quickfox Publishing
www.quickfox.co.za

First edition 2024

#CONFIDENCE

ISBN: 978-0-7961-6968-6

Illustrations by Nicolene Louw
Cover design by Allendre Hine
Page design by Vanessa Wilson

Contents

1. Confidence matters

1.1 Introduction

> 'Once we believe in ourselves, we can risk curiosity, wonder, spontaneous delight, or any experience that reveals the human spirit.' **E.M. McMAHON**

I've always wondered why some people seem to ooze confidence from every pore and others, equally or even more competent, struggle to get past their own limiting beliefs and never shine. Over the past few years I have been researching and coaching confidence and this book is the result of what I have learnt.

A scientific study[1] suggests that somewhere between 25% and 40% of our confidence is due to the genes we inherit. Another big chunk stems from how we were raised. If we were encouraged as a child, we grew in confidence. If we were told we were useless or stupid or would never amount to anything, our confidence was destroyed and we struggle to get past that as an adult.

But the more encouraging story is that **a big part of confidence is a skill that can be learnt**. If we don't have it, it doesn't mean we never will. **We can build it and boost it, bit by bit.**

Every small success will grow your confidence, and that will lift your performance, which will result in greater success. That success will develop your confidence further and then, caught up in this virtuous circle, there will be no stopping you!

I have taken all that I learnt as a business leader and as a coach and all that I have studied in Positive Psychology and distilled it all into 48 hacks, or what I call building blocks. Like little LEGO® blocks, these stack together to build confidence – small wins that will add up over time to a big difference.

... A BIG PART OF CONFIDENCE IS A SKILL THAT CAN BE LEARNT ... WE CAN BUILD IT AND BOOST IT, BIT BY BIT.

Building confidence needs hard work, taking risks and learning from failures, but it is something we can all do. Whether it's standing up for yourself, following things through, doing the right thing, ignoring what others think, or breathing properly, there are many, many ways to increase your confidence. I've set them out in four sections:

- Building yourself;
- Building your social life;
- Building your career, and
- Building your future.

You don't have to work through the book. Dip in and out. Just small changes in any area will add up. Armed with coffee, courage and confidence, you can conquer the world!

> 'Your success will be determined by your own confidence and fortitude.'
>
> **MICHELLE OBAMA**

1.2 Why confidence counts

> 'If you're presenting yourself with confidence, you can pull off pretty much anything.' **KATY PERRY**

Why is confidence important? Two big reasons:

1. Confidence beats competence. Confidence is a bigger predictor of success than ability. (That sucks, I know.)

2. Confidence leads to action. With it, you are more willing to learn new things, to embrace new ideas and to keep on working to achieve what you want.

There are as many definitions of confidence as there are stars in the sky, but most people agree that confidence consists of two elements – a belief in your ability to reach your goals, which the psychologists call self-efficacy, and a belief that the future will turn out well, which the psychologists call optimism.

A belief in your own abilities is knowing that you are competent to achieve what you are aiming for. It's a quiet but firm belief in your abilities. It's also recognising your weaknesses and acting accordingly. You believe that you can learn new skills and solve the problems the world dishes up to you. Self-efficacy must be realistic; you don't want to believe you'll be the next *Idols* champion if you can't hold a tune.

Optimism is a positive mindset. It is the belief that, on balance, things will turn out okay. Professor Martin Seligman, the founder of Positive Psychology, talks about our explanatory style,[2] which is the way we think about the causes of things that happen in our lives. The pessimists believe that things will continue to be bad; it's their own fault when things go wrong; the world is full of bad people and horrible events. If you think like that, you can't be confident about reaching your goals and you aren't going to put in the effort needed for success. Optimists believe they can improve, that negative events are often just bad luck and that they won't last. Optimists believe that they have talent and that they will succeed.

OPTIMISM IS A POSITIVE MINDSET.
IT IS THE BELIEF THAT, ON BALANCE,
THINGS WILL TURN OUT OKAY.

'Confidence makes individuals appear more competent in the eyes of others, even when that confidence is unjustified and unwarranted,'[3] according to Professor Cameron Anderson, from the Haas School of Business at the University of California. Scientific evidence shows that 'fake it till you make it' can work, although you will see it's not a strategy I recommend.

We've all seen brash over-confident folk dominating conversations, interrupting people, insisting they are correct, boasting about their achievements. But real confidence isn't based on bluster or wishful thinking or inflated egos, but on skills, authenticity, self-belief and an optimistic outlook.

What does having confidence get you?

- Better performance
- Resilience
- Better relationships
- Openness to try new things
- An end to procrastinating

> 'Life is not easy for any of us. But what of that? We must have perseverance and above all confidence in ourselves. We must believe that we are gifted for something and that this thing, at whatever cost, must be attained.'
>
> **MADAME MARIE CURIE**

2. Building you

2.1 Your life mosaic

> 'Never get so busy making a living that you forget to make a life.'
>
> **DOLLY PARTON**

Not having balance in your life can bite you badly. Working 24/7 may bring career and financial rewards but sooner or later you're going to feel the hollowness of missing out. How satisfied you are with all the aspects of your life? Take a few minutes to fill in this Wheel of Life. Look at each dimension and score your satisfaction with it out of a possible 10, with 10 being the highest. Does your wheel look wonky!? You can't work flat out 24/7 indefinitely nor subject yourself to endless stress without getting to burnout. Is that where you are heading? Which parts of your wheel needs attention?

This is a completed example:

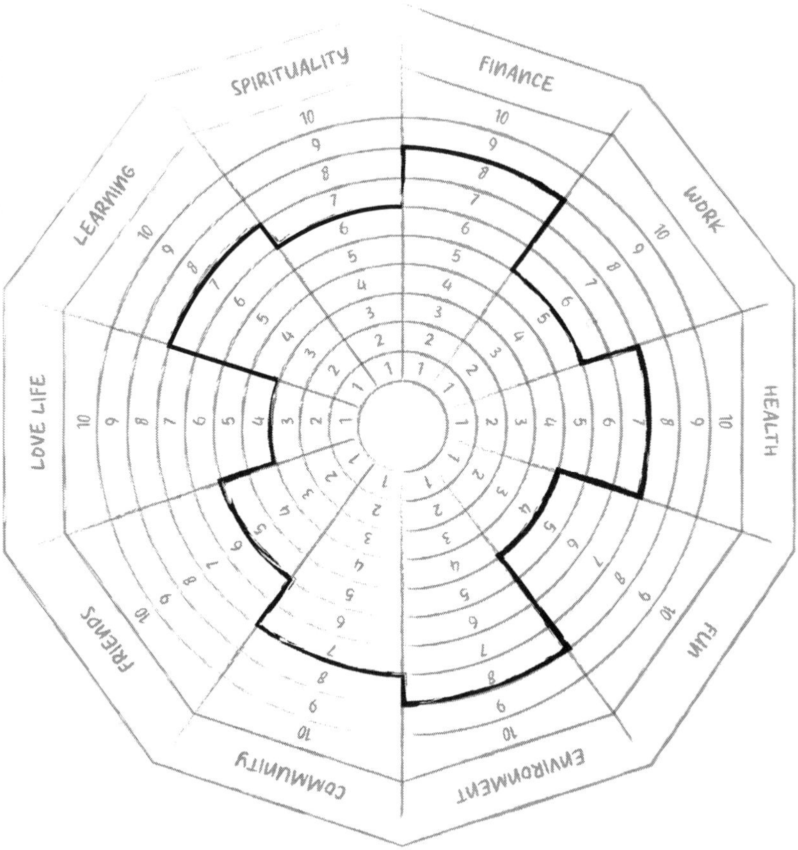

Here's a blank one for you to complete and you can choose which aspects of your life you want to score:

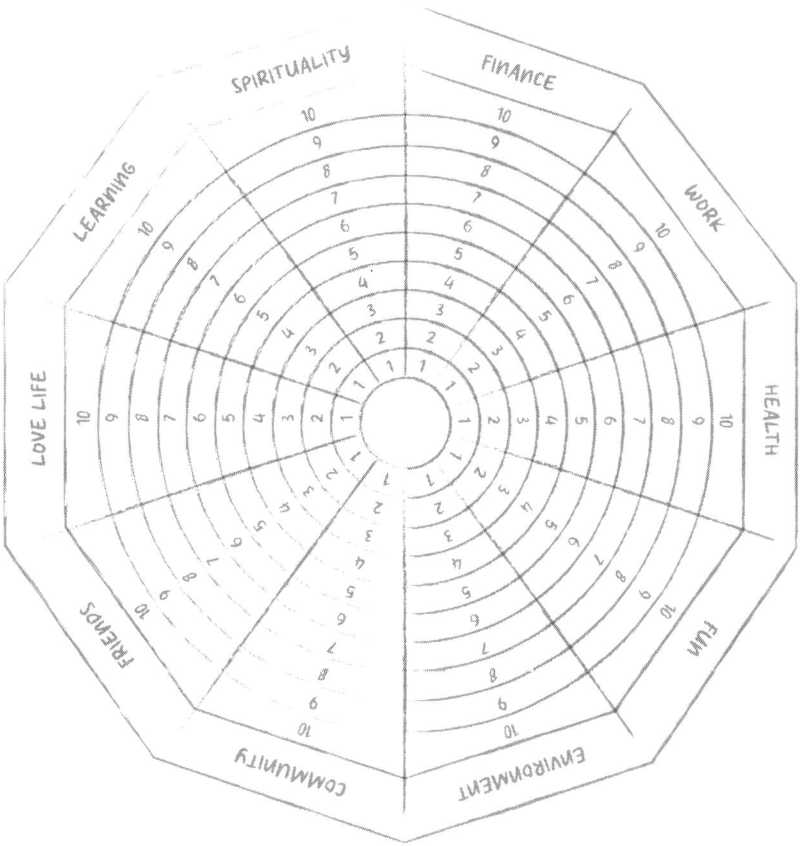

Everybody is different and what makes for harmony in your life might well be chaos for someone else. Sadhguru, the famous Indian spiritual teacher says that there is no such thing as work-life balance – it is all life. The balance has to be within you.

Another way to look at your life is to see it as a mosaic. All the different elements in your life – work, play, family, friends, partners, religion, values, community – are pieces in your mosaic. Some are big, some are broken. Some are shiny, some are dull. They are all different sizes and colours but they all make up your picture. If your work piece is too big and too dark, it will spoil the beauty of your life mosaic. So, take the time to step back and look at and like what you are creating.

> ALL THE DIFFERENT ELEMENTS IN YOUR LIFE – WORK, PLAY, FAMILY, FRIENDS, PARTNERS, RELIGION, VALUES, COMMUNITY – ARE PIECES IN YOUR MOSAIC

We are often scared to limit our work hours, but have you thought that doing that could perhaps mean you'll achieve more? It is interesting that in the last few years big companies have been experimenting with introducing four-day working weeks and finding that their employees are as productive as they were working five days.[4] They also find that employees are happier. Staff use the fifth day to spend time with their family, go shopping or volunteer for charity work.

If your family and friends are demanding too much of you, learn to set boundaries. Practise saying 'no' or 'I'd love to help you but I can't.' If work is demanding too much from you, and you're not happy about it, summon up the courage to speak up and say so. Set limits on the hours you are prepared to answer emails after work. Build times in your life that you can just be still. As Michelle Obama says: 'We need to do a better job of putting ourselves higher on our own "to do" list.'

Make a drawing of your own life mosaic. Do you like it?

> 'We are mosaics – pieces of light, love, history, stars – glued together with magic and music and words.'
>
> **ANITA KRISHAN**

2.2 Integrity

> 'Integrity is choosing courage over comfort; choosing what is right over what is fun, fast, or easy; and choosing to practise our values rather than simply professing them.'
>
> **BRENÉ BROWN**

Integrity is like the flat, green LEGO® board that kids use as a base for building something with the other blocks. **Integrity and authenticity together are the foundation for building confidence**.

With integrity, you keep your promises. You do what you say you will do. You and your word are one and the same and when you commit to doing something, there is a power in that commitment that propels you toward achieving your goals. For example, if you commit to delivering a report by Friday, and you have integrity, the energy of that commitment will help ensure that you deliver on time.

INTEGRITY AND AUTHENTICITY TOGETHER ARE THE FOUNDATION FOR BUILDING CONFIDENCE.

You follow through and you follow up.

If you have integrity, you don't have to question yourself or your actions. It is about doing the right thing, even when no one is there to see you. What you say is what you do – you are impeccable with your word. If you take responsibility for yourself and don't make promises that you can't or won't keep, you build a core of self-respect that is very powerful.

Obviously, life happens and sometimes you do end up breaking your word, but then you need to apologise wholeheartedly. This applies at work, in your relationships and especially with children.

What does integrity mean to you?

- ☺ What does it feel like when you don't keep your word?
- ☺ What does it feel like when you do?
- ☺ How do you feel when people around you have no integrity?
- ☺ How can integrity increase your confidence?
- ☺ Do your friends trust you to keep your word?

> IT IS ABOUT DOING THE RIGHT THING, EVEN WHEN NO ONE IS THERE TO SEE YOU. WHAT YOU SAY IS WHAT YOU DO – YOU ARE IMPECCABLE WITH YOUR WORD.

There is a bigger picture. Integrity is also used in the sense of being whole, undivided and complete. For example, we talk of the integrity of databases when we refer to a set of data as being consistent and accurate over time. That idea of the whole means that we should all aim to be incorruptible, trustworthy and dependable because we are all part of the bigger whole – our society – that will only function properly if we all have integrity.

It's not easy. Integrity can be really challenging. Integrity can come with a big price, as whistle-blowers often know to their cost.

Examples of broken integrity

- Reading someone's private emails without their permission.
- Saying you trust someone and then secretly checking their WhatsApp feed.
- Agreeing to babysit and then cancelling when you're unexpectedly asked out.
- Promising to visit your grandparents over the weekend and then not showing up.
- Always being late for meetings.
- Delivering work you know is second-rate.
- Agreeing to do something at work and then, at the last minute, saying you are too busy.
- Leaking confidential information.
- Missing deadlines that you accepted.

> 'One of the truest tests of integrity is its blunt refusal to be compromised.'
>
> **CHINUA ACHEBE**

2.3 True to you

> 'Find out who you are and be that person. That's what your soul was put on this earth to be. Find that truth, live that truth and everything else will come.' **ELLEN DEGENERES**

Calling someone two-faced is a hard-hitting insult. None of us like the person who says one thing to one person and something else to another, who changes their story depending on their audience.

Authenticity partners with integrity as the foundation for building self-confidence. Because you can't be confident in yourself if you aren't comfortable with who you are.

You may have read the saying: 'Be yourself. Everyone else is taken.' It's incorrectly attributed to the writer Oscar Wilde but he did write: 'Most people are other people. Their thoughts are someone else's opinions, their lives a mimicry, their passions a quotation.'

Authenticity is about who you really are, not the image you would like to project or the someone else you'd like to be. It's becoming your own person, the result of a lifelong process of learning about yourself. And to be authentic, you need to have a hard think about who you are.

Here's a checklist to help you begin to find your authentic self:

Ask yourself:

- ☺ What 10 things do I know to be true?
- ☺ What are my values?
- ☺ What are my beliefs?
- ☺ What am I good at?
- ☺ What is important to me?
- ☺ What are the three things that I do that define me?
- ☺ Do I know and accept myself?
- ☺ Does my social media image reflect the real me?
- ☺ Who do I really want to be?

Once you have a feel for your intrinsic self-worth you can stop playing the roles that your family has given you or that social media is spelling out for you. If you try to be someone you aren't, you are telling yourself that who you are is not okay. There are so many assigned roles that make for inauthentic lives – it's exhausting and painful trying to live up to them. Don't do it**. Just be you.**

Some of society's stereotypes that we don't need to accept:

- the macho man
- the male provider
- the wonder woman with a fabulous career and a perfect family
- the dutiful daughter
- the loving wife and homemaker
- the faithful spouse
- the inspiring teacher
- the perfect body
- the diligent mother
- the fabulous cook
- the witty entertainer
- the tireless organiser
- the conscious citizen

In the book *The Confidence Code*[5], the authors write: 'Confidence comes from stepping out of your comfort zone and working towards goals that come from your own values and needs, goals that aren't determined by society.'

A note of caution. I have seen colleagues behaving very badly, insulting people because they believe they are being authentic in saying what they think. Bad manners and authenticity can't live in the same space. That kind of behaviour will undermine any rapport you have built up with your friends or colleagues, leaving you isolated and eroding your confidence.

> 'When confidence emanates from our core, we are at our most powerful.' **THE CONFIDENCE CODE**[6]

2.4 No more knights

> 'If you are searching for the one person who will change your life forever, look in the mirror.'
>
> **AUTHOR UNKNOWN**

Do you know people who are always deep in a crisis caused by themselves but who always expect a knight in shining armour to come to their rescue and make everything okay again? Daddy will pay. My colleague will sort it out. My boyfriend will fix it.

Accountability means that we take responsibility for our own lives.

Many people are quick to blame other people for what has gone wrong – they believe they are never to blame. Bad things do happen to people but, even where blaming others is justified, it won't help to stay stuck as a victim because then you are giving up on being in charge of your own life.

> ACCOUNTABILITY MEANS THAT WE TAKE RESPONSIBILITY FOR OUR OWN LIVES.

We make our own choices and we must live with the results. Until we accept that we are the agents of our own successes or failures, we won't have self-respect or confidence in ourselves.

Here are some ways you can be accountable – what can you add to the list?

- ☺ Doing the right thing for the business.
- ☺ Being on time.
- ☺ Meeting deadlines.
- ☺ Contributing your ideas.
- ☺ Supporting your colleagues.

- Owning up to mistakes.
- Organising your finances.
- Paying your debts.
- Contributing your share.

We all make mistakes but the worst thing you can do at work (or in life generally) is to try and hide them, pretend they never happened, blame someone else or come up with a million excuses. Or expect that someone else will rescue you from the mess you've made. Everyone will respect you far more if you own up, apologise, and then get on with whatever it is you need to do to sort the problem out.

Complaining is another trap. We can grumble endlessly about how we never have time to get to the gym, how the shops make clothes so tight these days, how we can't lose weight because we have a slow metabolism – but nothing changes the situation. The only way is to get real, accept responsibility, eat better and exercise more.

> 'I am the master of my fate. I am the captain of my soul.' ***INVICTUS* BY WILLIAM ERNEST HENLEY**

2.5 It's your choice

> 'The most influential person in your life is you.' **MEL ROBBINS**

In 1944, when Holocaust survivors Edith Eger and her sister arrived at Auschwitz, they were given prison clothes to wear and their hair was shorn. Edith's sister had been feted as a beauty and she turned to her sister to ask: 'How do I look?' Edith thought she looked like a mangy dog, but she needed to find an answer. 'Your eyes,' she told her sister, 'they're so beautiful. I never noticed them when they were covered up by all that hair.' 'Thank you,' her sister whispered. Edith, who much later became a psychologist, wrote in her autobiography[7] that it was the first time she realised that we have a choice between paying attention to what we have lost or paying attention to what we still have.

> WE HAVE A CHOICE BETWEEN PAYING ATTENTION TO WHAT WE HAVE LOST OR PAYING ATTENTION TO WHAT WE STILL HAVE.

It's annoying when some of the self-help gurus say that you can choose to be happy. It's not that simple; the happy part isn't always possible, although the choosing bit is. Horrible things happen. Things that you can't control. You can choose how to react though, even when happiness isn't in the equation.

When life is tough:

- ☺ You can choose to focus on other things.
- ☺ You can choose to keep busy.
- ☺ You can choose to keep exercising.
- ☺ You can search for positives, even small ones.
- ☺ You can practise gratitude, even though it's hard.
- ☺ You can choose optimism.

To quote Edith Eger again: 'My own search for freedom and my years as a clinical psychologist have taught me that suffering is universal ... But victimhood is optional.'[7]

Our life doesn't just happen. It is shaped and defined by the choices we make. We don't get to make many choices as a child, but as adults we choose where we live, what work we do, who our partners are, all the way through to what we eat.

If we take responsibility for our choices and don't blame outside forces, we have control over our lives. We have the freedom to choose compassion, laughter, curiosity, humility, to make a difference.

Importantly we can make choices about how we respond when someone tries to undermine our confidence. Lashing out in anger or retreating into our shells doesn't serve us well, so we need to take time to choose our response. We can acknowledge our feelings of hurt but then choose a strategy to solve the problem or to change that person's view.

IF WE TAKE RESPONSIBILITY FOR OUR CHOICES AND DON'T BLAME OUTSIDE FORCES, WE HAVE CONTROL OVER OUR LIVES.

Take time before reacting – think about your choice. In his book, *Man's Search for Freedom*, Victor Frankel wrote: 'Between stimulus and response there is a space that is our power to choose our response. In our response lies our growth and freedom.'

(A caution – if you have suffered trauma as a child or adult and are battling to move forward, please get professional counselling. Choosing a positive way may be much harder for you.)

> 'I am not what happened to me, I am what I choose to become.' **CARL JUNG**

2.6 The evil twins: 'if/then' and 'when, then.'

> 'Be content with what you have; rejoice in the way things are. When you realise there is nothing lacking, the whole world belongs to you.'
>
> **LAO TZU**

Do you recognise any of these?

'If I lost 5kg, then I'd feel beautiful.'
'If I get a boob job, then he'll love me more.'
'If my partner was more affectionate, I'd be more loving.'
'When I get that BMW, then I'll be happy.'
'When I get a better job, then I know my problems will be over.'

Don't postpone happiness for 'if' and 'when' – they may never happen. And if or when they do, you may well be disappointed and you'll start again – looking for a new 'when' or a new 'if.'

> DON'T POSTPONE HAPPINESS FOR 'IF' AND 'WHEN' – THEY MAY NEVER HAPPEN.

A big part of the problem is social media, which constantly suggest that we need more – whether it's better running shoes, a designer outfit, expensive make-up or a new leather couch. The momentary pleasure of shopping disappears, leaving us with more stuff and less money.

Purchases rarely make us happier for long, partly because we get used to them so quickly – what the psychologists call habituation or hedonic adaptation. The result is that discontent is always sitting on our shoulder, making suggestions as to what else we could buy or do to feel better.

Studies have shown that if you are going to spend money, rather spend it on experiences, because the anticipation and retelling of them will make you far happier than buying more stuff.[8] Spending time or money, however little the amount, on random acts of kindness has also been shown to make you happier.

And the new partner who will change your life? You will find that magical person one day but you can't mope around for the next few years waiting for him or her to show up. When you are contented, you are more likely to attract people, so aim to **be happy in yourself and happy with yourself.**

If we make our happiness dependent on someone or something external, then we're not in control. When we take responsibility for our own happiness, we feel the confidence of knowing **'I am enough'** and that shines through. One way to do that is to shift our focus to what we already do have and be grateful for that.

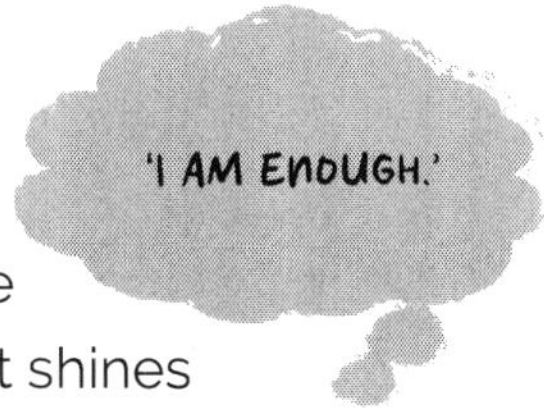

When you're itching to shop?

When you feel the need to hop online to buy because you are feeling down, an instant 'feel better' solution is simply to GET OUT AND ABOUT! (See 2.14)

Go for a walk – ideally in nature, but around your city block if that's all there is. And on your walk, find 10 things that interest, amuse or delight you. When you're back, you'll feel better.

> 'If you want to feel rich, just count the things you have that money can't buy'. **UNKNOWN**

2.7 You are not your emotions

> 'But feelings can't be ignored, no matter how unjust or ungrateful they seem.' **ANNE FRANK**

We all have loads of different emotions every day. Irritated by a rude shop assistant. Happy because we met an old friend. Anxious about our bank balance. Angry over a hurtful remark. Sad to see a homeless person. Excited to be invited to a party.

Everyone's emotions come and go, but what are emotions?

Modern neuroscience has found that emotions are processes performed by our brain.

Our brains are influenced by evolution and by our own individual experiences over the years.

With emotion, the brain instantaneously picks up that there are now internal bodily changes, however minuscule, such as an increased heart rate or quicker breathing, and it scans the external environment to check what it is we are seeing or hearing or sensing or smelling. As it does that scan, it also instantly connects it to previous behaviours and knowledge. The result is an emotion – a pattern of neural activity which co-ordinates inputs from external senses and bodily states and helps us respond.

If we see an old flame, our heart begins to beat faster without our even knowing it, our eyes instantly relay to our brain who we are seeing and the brain immediately checks in with all the stored memories, and the instantaneous result is the emotion of anxiety or happiness or anger.

Looking at emotions as messages or data that are telling us that something is going on makes it easier to accept that we are not our emotions. We don't choose to have emotions, just as we don't decide in advance to think the thoughts that pop up in our heads. But for many of us negative emotions can be overwhelming and crippling. They go round and round in our heads – what the psychologists call ruminating. Suppressing them can do more harm than good, so here are some strategies to help:

How to deal with strong emotions

- Name the emotion, accept it and recognise that it won't last.
- Remind yourself that tomorrow you will probably feel differently.
- Visualise your mind as an animal like a shark or a tiger and then say to yourself something like 'This is my inner tiger eating away at me again, always freaking me out'. Suggesting that it isn't you doing the thinking makes the emotion less powerful.
- Put some distance between you and the emotion. Don't think 'I am an idiot' but rather think 'Well, that was an idiotic thing to do'; rather rephrase 'I am so useless' as 'I haven't yet done anything useful in this situation'.
- Try and identify what's triggering the emotion. Change the trigger if you can, or at least do something different – leave the room, go for a walk, play music through your headphones, recite a poem, watch a silly comedy.

- Practise self-compassion. Speak to yourself as if talking to a friend in a gentle, comforting way, acknowledge that you are doing the best you can to cope. Put both hands on your heart space and tell yourself that it is okay to have this feeling.
- Breathe slowly to calm yourself (see 3.6).
- Exercise and meditation significantly reduce negative thoughts and emotions.

Let's say you are feeling upset – for example, a project of yours has been rejected. Just stay with the emotion, accept that it is okay for now to be upset but know that by tomorrow the worst of this feeling will have passed. It is not a catastrophe (see 2.9). Now focus on something else, check your emails, buy an ice cream, play some loud music.

Being confident that you can manage your emotions makes you powerful.

> 'You are not your emotions. You have emotions. And you can master them.'
>
> **JOHN LENNON**

2.8 Bad news is bigger than good news

> 'Your mind is a ship; it can sail across the universe as long as you don't allow negative thoughts to sink it.'
>
> **MATSHONA DHLIWAYO**

Why do newspapers always lead with bad news? Why does criticism have more impact than praise? Why do we never forget the times we felt shamed?

It seems the brain is hardwired for negativity and this is most probably due to evolution. When we lived in caves, we needed to be constantly on the alert for possible dangers – enjoying the sunset wasn't a good idea if a wolf was lurking close by. The people who survived were those who concentrated on threats and fears and it's their genes we have inherited. It's called the negativity bias.

That's why we register negative stimuli quickly and dwell on them; why first bad impressions are lasting, and why we chew over supposed insults and don't forget them. We can easily remember the

criticisms we received in our last job review but barely remember the compliments and recognition. How daft is that? We all do it – it's how our brains are built. The fact is that negative information causes a stronger reaction in the cerebral cortex than positive or neutral information.[9]

Have you noticed that while bad news can easily upset a good mood, good news seldom changes a bad mood? Did you know that if people lose $100, they experience negative emotions that are stronger than their positive emotions if they win $100?

How to deal with this negativity bias:

- Once again, the answer lies in being mindful (see 2.12).
- Be aware of this negative bias.
- Deliberately think of happy times.
- Focus on good memories and on positive activities.
- Stop and savour enjoyable moments.
- When those negative thoughts pop up to undermine your confidence, imagine yourself crushing them underfoot. Or imagine packing them inside a big red balloon and watching it float skywards.

> 'Am I good enough?
> Yes, I am.'
>
> **MICHELLE OBAMA, *BECOMING*.**

2.9 Catastrophic thinking

> 'Of all your troubles great and small, the greatest are the ones that don't happen at all.' **THOMAS CARLYLE**

For some of us, negative thoughts take over, racing ahead to the future with a host of 'What if?' questions that torment us and eat away at our confidence. Thoughts like 'What if I fail?' 'What if this pain in my chest is a heart attack?' 'What if my partner leaves me?'

This is what a catastrophising thought pattern looks like:

- The business isn't doing well.
- What if I'm retrenched?
- And what if I can't get another job?
- And then I won't be able to pay my bond and I'll lose my house.
- And then I'll lose my car.
- And what if none of my family and friends can help me?
- I'll end up homeless. And then ...

Anxiety can be a useful emotion if it spurs us into action, but catastrophising is decidedly not helpful. When we ruminate endlessly, continually imagining irrational worst-case scenarios, it depletes our energy.

Our body's response to these negative thoughts is to switch into fight or flight mode because it can't distinguish between real and imaginary threats. Our body releases adrenalin to make our heart beat faster and shunts blood to our muscles. It also releases cortisol, a stress-related hormone that helps us utilise stored energy, which is great if we are running away from a sabre-toothed tiger, but not so great if we have a constant build-up of cortisol in our stressed-out bodies, weakening our immune systems.

Psychologists have identified three different styles of catastrophising. Do you recognise any of them?

- One is described as a downward spiral where story just gets worse and worse.

- A second is a scatter-shot style all sorts of different dreadful outcomes are generated.

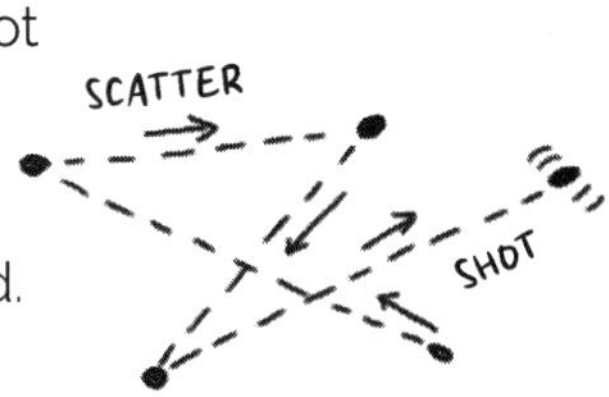

* And a third is called circling or ruminating, when one negative thought keeps going around and around in the brain.

The good news is that you can escape these thinking traps. How? The starting point is to immediately challenge them. Demand some hard evidence of what you are thinking; prove to yourself these thoughts aren't true.

- Say to yourself: 'That is not true because …'
- Then you can take a more optimistic perspective, saying: 'A more useful way to look at this problem is …' Try to reframe your thoughts (see 4.3).
- And then, make a plan. Take a second to stop, breathe and go forward with a plan such as 'If X happens, I will Y.'
- Your breathing is important because breathing deeply and slowly will restore your body's balance and help you think more clearly (see 3.6).

When you challenge your catastrophic thinking, writing things down will help you. Start with a short description of the problem and then draw three columns with the headings 'Worst-case Scenario', 'Probable Outcome' and 'Best Result', and fill in each column. Finally ask yourself 'What purposeful action can I take?'

Here's an example where you must give a presentation to the board and you are consumed with anxiety.

WORST-CASE SCENARIO	PROBABLE OUTCOME	BEST RESULT
I'll start shaking. I'll dry up. I'll look stupid. I'll get my figures mixed up. I have the wrong data. People won't listen to me. I won't be able to answer the questions. I'll be demoted.	The board members listen politely. They ask difficult questions. I can answer most of them. My director supports me. I am asked to revise certain recommendations and bring the report back to the next board meeting for approval.	I present confidently and with positive energy. The board members listen carefully. They ask good questions. They agree with my conclusions. They support my proposals. They allocate the budget. I get recognition for my ideas.

Take time imagining the best result. And once you've drawn up one of these charts, do whatever it is you need to do to get that best result. In the example above, the action could be to do a dry run with colleagues or practise in front of the mirror.

What do I do when I'm in this space? I tell myself three things: 'No one has died. The world has not stopped turning. Now let's make a plan.'

> 'Put your thoughts to sleep.
> Do not let them cast a shadow
> over the moon of your heart.
> Let go of thinking.' **RUMI**

2.10 Powerful words

> 'Words have a magical power. They can bring either the greatest happiness or the deepest despair.'
>
> **SIGMUND FREUD**

The old folks used to say: 'Sticks and stones can break your bones, but words can never harm you.' That's nonsense. It's words we remember, especially the ones that hurt us. Words can evoke emotions; they can get people to act and even change how people think. Choosing the right words is important. It isn't about good grammar and vocabulary but about the power that is in the words you use.

IT ISN'T ABOUT GOOD GRAMMAR AND VOCABULARY BUT ABOUT THE POWER THAT IS IN THE WORDS YOU USE.

AND not BUT

If you want to kill someone's enthusiasm stone dead, use the word 'but'. If someone interrupts you with a 'but', that's what you remember because the negative is what stays with you (see 2.8). Look at the difference in positive and negative impact between these pairs of sentences:

- 'You did a great job on this report but the layout needs improving' **versus** 'You did a great job on this report and I think you can tweak the layout to also make it look amazing.'
- 'This is a great idea but we don't have the budget' **versus** 'This is a great idea and let's see if we can afford it.'

Using 'and' is an affirmation that you have heard what someone is saying and that you value them. It's a sure way to keep a conversation going, yet we all use 'but' all the time.

SOME not ALL/NONE

The words 'all' and 'none' suggest that there is nothing that can be done. Using 'some' will give a more relaxed perspective when you are catastrophising (see 2.9). Instead of 'Everything is going wrong' think 'Some things are going wrong.'

Generalisations also don't help in good communication because they aren't true, e.g. 'All men are cheats', 'All politicians are corrupt' or 'All whites are racists'.

YOU'RE RIGHT not I KNOW

Saying 'I know' to someone is a big dampener, especially if they are sharing something they have just found out for themselves. If you say: 'Yes, you're right', you come across positively and the other person feels good.

YET not CAN'T

'Yet' is an important part of a growth mindset (see 4.14) and it's so powerful. I love that it has become such a key word in the vocabulary of good teachers. But it's not just for children – it is useful in the way we talk to ourselves and how we internalise confidence. Look at how these sentences are transformed by adding 'yet' to them:

'I can't do this ... *yet*.'
'This doesn't work ... *yet*.'
'I don't know ... *yet*.'
'I don't get it ... *yet*.'
'I'm not good at this ... *yet*.'
'I haven't had a promotion ... *yet*.'

LEARNING not FAILING

Replace the word 'failing' with 'learning' in your vocabulary. Think about 'I'm failing Statistics at Uni' versus 'I'm learning Statistics at Uni.'

HAVE TO versus WANT TO

When you replace 'have to' with 'want to', the words make chores seem less challenging. Try 'I want to cook supper' rather than 'I have to cook supper'.

ASKING QUESTIONS

Have you ever given a presentation or summed up a meeting and then asked: 'Do you have any questions?' and had everyone stare blankly or look down at their notes? Try phrasing it as 'What questions do you have?' – you're much more likely to get some.

A university lecturer told us that when she switched from asking 'Does anyone have a question before I move on?' to 'Someone ask me a question before I move on', it was a game-changer.

It can help to be direct when you need something. Instead of asking 'Does anyone have a pen?' ask 'Who has a pen?'

Another great question that can open doors and build relationships is: 'Can I ask your advice?' You'll be surprised at how many people are happy to help.

Use these phrases more often:

- I need your help.
- Can I ask your advice?
- I'm sorry.
- Thank you.
- What can I do?
- I get how you are feeling.

> 'Be careful with your words. Once they are said, they can only be forgiven, not forgotten.' **UNKNOWN**

2.11 Your superpower

> 'Today you are You, that is truer than true, there is no one alive that is Youer than You.' **DR SEUSS**

You have a superpower. I call it your FU power and it is based on your knowing that there is only one you in the universe. Only you can do what you do the way you do it. Only you see the world through your eyes. And that gives you your unique power.

So, with that knowledge, your FU power must develop an FU attitude for when you need it.

An FU attitude is staring your adversary or detractor in the eye as you smile sweetly. You roll your eyes marginally upwards, perhaps narrow them slightly or maybe lift your eyebrows the tiniest bit. You look at him or her long enough for them to feel uncomfortable. Most importantly, you don't say anything. Inside you are thinking 'FU'. You and the other person now both know you mean business.

... THERE IS ONLY ONE YOU IN THE UNIVERSE. ONLY YOU CAN DO WHAT YOU DO THE WAY YOU DO IT.

Silence is incredibly powerful. It makes people seriously uncomfortable. They rush to say something to fill the gap. And if you say something in that moment, you will ruin the effect and, besides, you might say something you will regret.

You need to practise this look in the mirror. Your FU is not the surly stare an angry teenager gives a parent. It is not a sneer, or a curled lip or a tight-lipped grin. It is a stare, with unblinking eyes. Your smile is soft but it doesn't reach your eyes. Everyone's FU attitude is a little different, but as long as it says 'I'm powerful and you are despicable', it will be a superpower.

This is the look you bring out when you know the resistance to your ideas is resistance to you rather than your actual ideas. It's the look you use when someone makes a sexist or racist remark. It's the look you give when someone you're not interested in makes a pass at you. It's the look you have when someone makes a rude personal remark about you. It's the look you bring out when a colleague makes a spectacularly stupid remark. But because you are smiling and staying quiet, no one can accuse you of being rude or cheeky or insubordinate.

Don't use the FU power too often. It will lose its power if it is seen as your usual attitude. Use it when everyone is expecting you to explode. It needs the element of surprise.

> 'The things that make us different, those are our superpowers'. **LENA WAITHE**

2.12 Meditation and mindfulness

> 'Where there is peace and meditation, there is neither anxiety nor doubt.' **ST FRANCIS DE SALES**

Meditation helps us feel whole and balanced, so if you're not already practising it, give it a go. Meditation will steady you and help you develop a more peaceful mind. Try to make it part of your routine. It doesn't have to be a lengthy practice – even just 10 minutes a day will make a difference after a few weeks.

By meditating regularly, you can become much more present, mindful and content. And that's the link to confidence. **Being contented, with a calmer mind, means that you will be more focused, less fearful and more confident**.

You can meditate anywhere provided it is quiet. Sit up straight, close your eyes and focus on your breathing. Thoughts will keep popping into your mind but let them drift away by not focusing on them. If you are struggling, download a meditation app – there are loads of super ones.

A form of meditation called Loving Kindness Meditation[10] can give you a big boost in feeling positive, making connections and being kind. You begin with a normal meditation and imagine that you're breathing out stress and breathing in peace and love. Then repeat some positive phrases to yourself. Phrases like 'May I be happy', 'May I be safe', 'May I be healthy', 'May I experience gratitude today', 'May I be confident today'. Sit quietly and allow these feelings to embrace you. Then think of those you care about and one by one visualise yourself repeating these or other loving phrases to them: 'Lindi, may you be happy. Lindi, may you be healthy' ... etc.

BEING CONTENTED, WITH A CALMER MIND, MEANS THAT YOU WILL BE MORE FOCUSED, LESS FEARFUL AND MORE CONFIDENT.

If you have had a torrid day and feel overwhelmed, try this meditation from the Buddhist monk, Thich Nhat Hahn.

It's more of a breathing exercise combined with a poem. While you are breathing, recite this to yourself:

> 'In, out
> Deep, slow
> Calm, ease
> Smile, release
> Present moment, wonderful moment.'

So, for each line say the first word as you breathe in, the second word as you breathe out. You can repeat each line as many times as you like. The effect is magical.

And if you find meditation is impossible, then walk instead, but be present as you walk (see 2.14).

The busier you are, the more you need bits of quiet time. Try to find a few quiet minutes during the day, every day, so that you can recharge and refocus.

Mindfulness is about being in the moment, paying attention to what we are experiencing now and being open to what is around us. Did you know that the mind is wandering 47% of the time?[11] And the mind wanders to the past and to the future but never to the present. This is called the Default Mode Network (DMN) of your brain and it kicks in the minute you stop focusing on something. You start thinking about things that happened in the past, things that might happen in the future and things that most probably will never happen at all.

And a wandering mind is not a happy one according to research by Harvard psychologists Killingsworth and Gilbert.[12] Their research shows that we are happiest when we're thinking about what we are doing. It is better to daydream about pleasant possibilities than unpleasant ones, but the happiest scenario is not to be daydreaming at all. Apparently, a person who is cooking supper and thinking about their cooking is happier than a person who is cooking and thinking about their weekend.

> ... WE ARE HAPPIEST WHEN WE'RE THINKING ABOUT WHAT WE ARE DOING.

> Buddha was asked: 'What have you gained from meditation?'
> He replied: 'Nothing! However, let me tell you what I lost: anger, anxiety, depression, insecurity, fear of old age and death.'

2.13 Gratitude

> 'Gratitude turns what we have into enough.' **AESOP**

It is clear from all the studies[13, 14] that **gratitude practices make a happier you, a healthier you and a better you**. Why? Because it builds new neural pathways in your brain as you focus on positive thoughts rather than on what is wrong in your life.

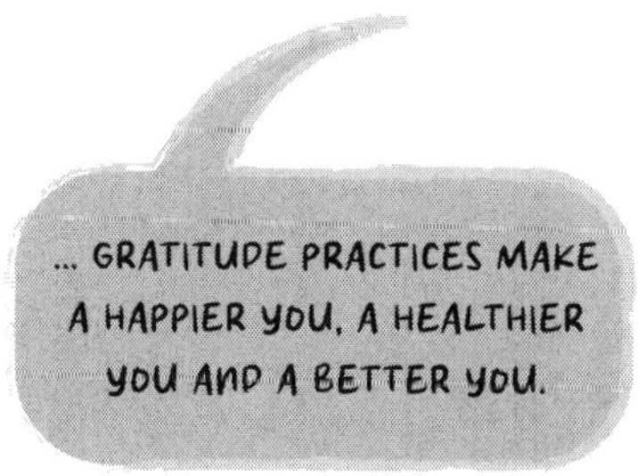

As we saw in 2.6, hedonic adaptation is the term the psychologists use for our quickly growing used to an enjoyable experience or purchase and then finding that the sense of enjoyment fades into the background and is forgotten. Practising gratitude can counteract this because you deliberately focus on what is good in your life rather than taking it for granted. So instead of getting used to your new car within a week or two of buying it, you continue to savour how good it smells, how comfortable it is, how neat the gadgets are, how fast it accelerates, how easily it parks.

You can't be two things at once – it's not possible to be thinking about positive things and be desperately sad at the same time. So, gratitude builds the capacity to cope with negative emotions.

And what does gratitude do for confidence? It's yet another building block. When you feel grateful, you often feel that you have benefited from another person's generosity, and this makes you feel valued and increases your self-esteem. In turn, gratitude inspires you to be more generous, kind and helpful to others, which will strengthen your business and social relationships.

In a 2015 study,[15] researchers found that university students who were inclined to be grateful had higher self-esteem and that, in turn, meant higher levels of wellbeing.

... GRATITUDE BUILDS THE CAPACITY TO COPE WITH NEGATIVE EMOTIONS.

So how do you practise gratitude? Here are some of the most popular ways:

Keep a gratitude journal. Write down or share thoughts about the positive things, the gifts you've received each day. Writing is recommended, but families might like to build the habit together by sharing with each other around the dinner table or at bedtime.

Three good things. At the end of every day, take time to reflect on at least three good things that happened that day. Set a reminder on your phone and have it ping you every night at the same time. It only takes a minute to come up with three good things for the day, and usually there are a lot more.

Write a thank-you note. One of the early gratitude studies showed how writing a letter of gratitude positively shifted students' sense of wellbeing. This makes you feel good, and imagine how good the recipient feels!

Mental subtraction. Think about how your life would look if you lost the things you value like your home or your health or your friends. Think about how you would feel if you had never achieved anything – never passed an exam nor had a salary increase. Celebrate these achievements by thinking what you would be without them. In one research project, people who imagined what life would be like without their romantic partner later reported that they felt more satisfied with their relationship.[16]

Pray. If you are religious, prayer is a perfect medium for gratitude.

Meditate. Take some time at the start of your meditation to focus on your blessings.

> 'Be thankful for what you have; you'll end up having more. If you concentrate on what you don't have, you will never, ever have enough.'
>
> **OPRAH WINFREY**

2.14 Forest bathing

> 'In nature, nothing is perfect and everything is perfect.' **ALICE WALKER**

Find a place. A forest. A park. A garden. Then make time. Turn off everything electronic. You now have all you need – silence and trees.

Be still. Savour nature – be present to all you can see, all you can hear, all you can smell, all you can touch. The tiny insects scurrying across the earth, the spider's web glistening in the sun, the sighs of the pines as they move in the wind, the feel of the tree's rough bark on your hands, the unseen bird calling, the fragrance of the yellow wild flowers.

The Austrian poet, Rainer Maria Rilke, wrote: 'And so it is that most people have no idea how beautiful the world is and how much magnificence is revealed in the tiniest things, in some flower, in a stone, in tree bark, or in a birch leaf.'

This is what your mind and your soul crave. In Japan it is called forest bathing or *Shinrin-yoku*. Modern neuroscience has shown that spending time in nature can help calm your anxious thoughts, improve your creativity and increase your vitality and self-motivation. That isn't a surprise. The feelings that come from forest bathing are rooted deep in our ancestry – we were farmers for thousands of years, and before that we were hunter-gatherers. We've only been city dwellers for a few hundred years and have only been staring at screens for a few decades.

A recent study[17] by the University of California San Francisco Memory and Aging Center (MAC) showed that older adults who took weekly 15-minute 'awe walks' for eight weeks reported increased positive emotions and less distress in their daily lives. They experienced more wellbeing and felt more generous.

It's definitely worth finding a few hours a week to nourish yourself in nature – take a forest bath and experience the joy that the poet William Blake described over 200 years ago:

> 'When the green woods laugh with the voice
> of joy,
> And the dimpling stream runs laughing by;
> When the air does laugh with our merry wit,
> And the green hill laughs with the noise of it.'

The calm that these walks will bring you will restore what a difficult day or week has taken out of you, and help you feel confident to tackle the next challenge.

And, if you want to take the forest beauty a bit further, plant an indigenous tree and nurture it, knowing that one distant day little creatures or even someone like you will sit beneath its branches in awe and wonder.

> 'Everybody needs beauty as well as bread, places to play in and pray in, where nature may heal and give strength to body and soul.' **JOHN MUIR**

2.15 Ten powerful questions

There are some questions that don't need to be answered but still need to be asked. Those are the questions that challenge our position, prickle our curiosity or shift our thinking. There is never a right or a wrong answer, but thinking about them lights a little spark in our consciousness that can lead to great things.

They are the type of questions that coaches like to ask and I've listed 10 of them below. Do any of them resonate with you? Is there one that makes you go, 'Oh, okay – I need to think about that'? For some people finding 'their' question and writing about it in their journal really helps them clarify what they need to shift. For others, tucking the thought into their subconscious is enough for the question to linger in their complex brain and ultimately pop out as new ideas and solutions.

My favourite confidence question is: 'If not me, then who?' or, in other words, 'Why not me?' What is holding you back from saying yes, from going for the promotion, from sticking up your hand, from asking that person out on a date, from starting a side hustle?

My favourite life question is: 'Is what I am doing helping me or harming me?' We could ask this so many times in a day. 'Is yelling at the guy who cut me off in traffic harming or helping me?' 'Is another glass of wine helping or harming me?' 'Is lying slumped miserably on the couch helping or harming me?' 'Is endlessly flicking though social media helping or harming me?' 'Is constantly criticising my partner helping or harming me?'

And my favourite growth question is: 'What do I not know?' This question is a brake to slow me down from jumping into judgement mode. It is also a question to make me curious to learn more. My goal in life is to make this question essential to my being.

There is a way to ask questions that makes a big difference to how you will answer them. If your questions are open-ended, they will generate plenty of thoughts. For example, 'What would it be like to stop obsessing about being perfect?' rather than 'Why didn't I do that 100% perfectly?'

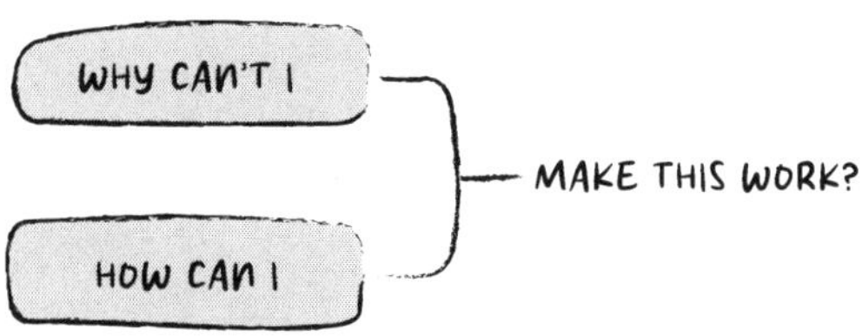

Here are 10 questions to think about:

- What's holding me back?
- If not me, then who?
- Is what I am doing helping or harming me?
- Do I need balance or boundaries?
- Why do I need everyone to like me?
- Is failing worse than doing nothing?
- What do I not know?
- Is there another way to look at this?
- What has this taught me?
- What if I can do this?

> 'Be willing to be a beginner every single morning.' **MEISTER ECKHARDT**

2.16 Ntshantsha's story

> 'People are more willing to help than you realise – all you have to do is ask.' **NTSHANTSHA**

If I was asked for three words to describe Ntshantsha Tafeni, I'd say grounded, focused and ambitious, yet, when you meet her, she comes across as anything but hardcore. What strikes you first is her quiet bearing and her beautiful glowing skin – living proof of the efficacy of her skincare range. Ntshantsha has been an entrepreneur since a young age and today is the founder and owner of Yivani® health and luxury beauty care products.

Born in a small town in the Eastern Cape, Ntshantsha was raised in a family of women. Moving schools for family reasons meant a poor matric result, and so she started working as a sales assistant, but within two years was making her own money by buying and selling clothes. *What gave you the courage to do that?* 'I had five aunts, my mother and my older sister who all had some sort of business going on and they were an inspiration and a source of informal mentoring.'

After six years, Ntshantsha had bigger dreams. 'I knew I didn't belong there, and so I had to go back to school to get a better matric.' And she did.
What was that like? Didn't you feel awkward?
'No, I felt no shame. I had my dreams and they had nothing to do with anyone else. And, ironically, I ended up being an inspiration to others to go back to school to finish or improve their matric.'

Armed with an excellent set of matric results, Ntshantsha got a bursary to study BCom at the University of the Western Cape. No one in her family had ever been to university but so many people helped and encouraged her. One of Ntshantsha's key business philosophies comes from this time. 'People are more willing to help than you realise – all you have to do is ask. We shouldn't work in silos.' And her inspiration to study hard and do well came from the conviction that 'If someone has done it, then I can do it.' Imagine the pride and jubilation on her graduation day when 20 family members came to Cape Town from the Eastern Cape to attend the ceremony

'IF SOMEONE HAS DONE IT, THEN I CAN DO IT.'

and to celebrate her landing an internship in South Africa's first new democratic parliament.

'I HAVE CONFIDENCE WHEN I KNOW WHAT I'M DOING, SO I ALWAYS WANT TO LEARN ...'

Ntshantsha says that working in parliament really boosted her confidence as she was working with South Africa's top leaders – democracy was new, everyone was keen to learn, to pull together and to help each other. She also built up a great network of contacts. When the internship was over, she landed a job in marketing at a company exporting fruit, and discovered that marketing was to become a lifelong passion. Her boss there encouraged her to grow and she moved on to a brand management job at Parmalat, and a few years later she embraced the challenge of moving to Johannesburg to work for Nestlé.

At Nestlé, Ntshantsha didn't just stick to marketing – she wanted to know more and so she asked to do a stint in sales and then in category management. *Why not stick to the area where you are successful?* 'I have confidence when I know what I'm doing, so I always want to learn; once you know all the aspects of a business, no one can push back and challenge you – they have respect.'

A lucrative offer and the desire to keep growing saw her join the fashion retailer, Edgars. Ntshantsha found the job a nightmare – at that time, brand managers were not rated while the buyers ruled supreme. Staff worked crazy long hours, which were never acknowledged, let alone appreciated. *What did you get out of the job?* 'I learnt resilience, to be really strong, to flourish outside of my comfort zone. Best of all, I decided that I wasn't going to be employed by anyone ever again.'

For the next few years Ntshantsha worked freelance as a project manager and consultant, doing whatever came her way, until one day she decided that she needed to focus on one thing and it should be something she loved – the healing tinctures and balms her grandmother used to make from plants harvested in the fields. It was time to start her own manufacturing company. *What gave you the confidence to do this?* 'I told myself: I've done brand building, new product development and project managing for other companies, why can't I do it for myself?

> 'I LEARNT RESILIENCE, TO BE REALLY STRONG, TO FLOURISH OUTSIDE OF MY COMFORT ZONE ...'

If I focus on this one thing, I can make it work. And you know what Mandela said: 'It always seems impossible until it's done.'

Ntshantsha has used all the lessons learnt in her working career in her own business – to tap into networks, to ask for information, to do lots of courses. She doesn't look for handouts but rather advice, and she connects with big businesses who are keen to help entrepreneurs. One of her heroes is Richard Branson who gave her the advice to recognise what she can do well and then to hire people to do the things she can't do. Right now, that means hiring someone to do social media while Ntshantsha focuses on production and new product development.

How did you keep going in tough times like Covid?
'I immediately saw an opportunity for change. Rather than focusing on products that were not selling, I converted my product lines to essential products like sanitisers, disinfectants, etc., and that is what saved the day.'

And your philosophy of life? 'I don't let people tell me anything about myself. I know what I can do. I believe in myself. I've always known I'll have my own business. And I work with communities of people where we can support each other. I love what I do – it doesn't feel like work.'And Ntshantsha's favourite quote?

> 'If you can dream it, you can do it.'
> **WALT DISNEY**

3.
Building your social life

3.1 Mirror, mirror on the wall

> 'Girls of all kinds can be beautiful – the thin, plus-sized, short, very tall, ebony to porcelain-skinned; the quirky, clumsy, shy, outgoing, and all in between. It's not easy though because many people still put beauty into a confining, narrow box ... Think outside of the box ... Pledge that you will look in the mirror and find the unique beauty in you.'
>
> **TYRA BANKS**

What is it about a mirror that it can undermine our confidence so easily? We look in the mirror and always find ourselves lacking – too fat, too thin, too wrinkled, too short, too freckled. The anxiety about our looks that we had as teenagers doesn't seem to disappear as we get older.

Most women want to change some aspect of how they look!

This body image stuff is important. How we see our bodies affects how we feel and think about ourselves and how we act. Women are much more concerned with their body image than men are and it has a huge influence on our self-confidence. A survey[18] of 3,300 girls and women across 10 countries revealed that 90% of all women aged 15 to 64 worldwide want to change at least one aspect of their physical appearance, with body weight ranking the highest. Women's anxiety about how they look is a global phenomenon. Two-thirds of women avoided doing some things such as giving an opinion, meeting friends, exercising, going to work, going to school, dating, and even going to the doctor – because they felt bad about their looks.

Advertising constantly tries to sell us beauty products. Social media bombards us with perfect images. When we compare ourselves to what we see on social media, we typically make upward comparisons, which make us feel worse. We compare ourselves to a perfectly curated, photoshopped, filter-applied myth. Social media is a make-believe world that undermines and destroys our confidence.

One way to break this mirror fixation is to acknowledge our insecurities about our body and then move on to celebrate our natural shape and size. We can think about what our bodies do for us – arms to hug with, feet to walk on, brains to think with. I love this post that came up on Twitter (X) from someone called Meg. Young Meg looks very pretty in the photo – she's cuddling a puppy – and appears to have quite big thighs. Here's what she wrote: 'To the men who choose to call me fat online. I'd rather have the body that I have and the soul that I have than be an adult, bullying people online. It doesn't faze me; says more about you than it does about me, babes, and the fatter my thighs, the more dogs can fit on them.' We must refuse to allow our negative ideas about our appearance to erode our confidence and limit our progress.

Women have an important role to play in building each other up and not allowing other women to constantly criticise their own body shape or that of other women. Remember men are rarely as critical of their own bodies and the irony is that most of them are not very critical of women's bodies either. They're looking at the bigger picture!

> 'I'm not the average girl from your video and I ain't built like a supermodel, but I learned to love myself unconditionally because I am a queen.' **INDIA ARIE**

3.2 Social anxiety – stop hugging the wall

> 'I wondered how many people there were in the world who suffered, and continued to suffer, because they could not break out from their own web of shyness and reserve, and in their blindness and folly built up a great distorted wall in front of them that hid the truth.'
>
> **DAPHNE DU MAURIER, REBECCA**

Do you dread going to parties or business events? Do you try to get out of going or hug the wall when you do? A lack of confidence in social settings can be crippling, stopping you from meeting new people and even limiting your career opportunities.

Time spent alone is rarely the cure for your blues – research shows you'd be happier if you connected with someone, even a stranger.[19] Starting conversations can be anxiety provoking and this makes people wonder and worry about what the people they've been talking to think of them. Other research[20] shows that after chatting, people from all walks of life systematically underestimated how much their conversation partners liked them and enjoyed their company. The researchers call this illusion 'The Liking Gap'. So, if you are shy, take comfort in knowing the person you spoke to liked the chat more than you thought.

There is even more comfort in a concept called 'The Spotlight Effect'. It's a psychological term for the tendency we all have to overestimate the degree to which other people are noticing us or our actions. You don't need to worry about whether people are looking at you – most times they aren't! If you think your hair is a mess or your outfit isn't right, remember most people simply won't notice.

Many people feel they don't have anything to talk about at social events. They feel totally excluded from conversation circles, always hovering on the edge and never knowing how to 'break in' to join the conversation. It helps to realise that **you don't have to be interesting, you just have to be interested.**

How to be part of a conversation

- Breathe! Try four-square breathing (3.6) before you walk into a social situation.
- Send a positive friendly message through your body language by sitting up or leaning in, smiling, nodding your head, looking interested.
- To join in a conversation, listen a while and then ask a question. Simple ones like 'How does that work?' 'What is it like when?' 'How did you feel?' work fine.
- To start a conversation, say hello, introduce yourself and then ask about the event or the people or the social situation. 'What did you think of that first speaker? Did you agree with him?' 'I know its John's birthday – do you know how old he is?' 'Isn't this food fabulous?'If you're sitting next to a stranger at a conference or a dining table, try starting the conversation with a compliment about their dress or tie or glasses. It's a good icebreaker.

- Don't freeze if someone asks you a question and you don't know the answer, or asks for your opinion and you don't have one. A simple 'I don't know' said with a smile is good enough.
- Be curious and interested in the other person. Ask questions and listen to the answers and then ask more questions based on those answers.

If you attend lots of social functions with some Very Important People, spend time beforehand googling the VIPs so that you can ask questions about their businesses or family or hobbies.

> 'You wouldn't worry so much about what others think of you if you realised how seldom they do.'
>
> **ELEANOR ROOSEVELT**

3.3 Just perfect?

> 'Perfectionism is a 20-ton shield that we lug around thinking it will protect us when, in fact, it's the thing that's really preventing us from taking flight.' **BRENÉ BROWN**

Perfectionism is about setting impossibly high standards for oneself. You would think high standards would be good for confidence, yet they can also end up being very damaging.

Perfectionism is punishing. Perfectionists are often their own harshest critics, beating up on themselves unnecessarily and crushing their confidence. You can be so obsessed with achieving perfection that you keep putting off getting started. Perfectionists don't like to take risks, yet avoiding them can stifle creativity.

Once you can accept your own vulnerability, you can let go of any obsession with perfectionism. If you are a person striving for excellence, great. But if you are trying to appear perfect all the time and to achieve unrealistic goals, that's not so great.

> ONCE YOU CAN ACCEPT YOUR OWN VULNERABILITY, YOU CAN LET GO OF ANY OBSESSION WITH PERFECTIONISM.

The kind of perfectionism that is problematic focuses on other people's expectations, and so the individual needs accomplishment to feel validated. But once a goal is achieved, perfectionists immediately replace it with yet another goal, not stopping to celebrate their success, and so they continue to struggle as their stress mounts with every new task.

What is it that makes us so scared to be vulnerable? We are afraid that others will judge us, will find us unworthy and then they will not want to be our partner, friend or colleague.

And because of that fear we hand over control to other people.

Yet if we own our story and our vulnerability and have the courage to be imperfect, we can cultivate the confidence to know we are enough.

Time and again I have learnt that 90% on any task is more than good enough. When you make peace with that, a huge amount of stress falls away.

It is liberating to accept your own imperfections. What does it matter if you can't dance well? Knowing this shouldn't stop you dancing. You don't need anyone's permission to have fun. Who cares what other people think? The truth is other people are never thinking about us as often as we think they are.

The famous American feminist, Gloria Steinem, taught us that 'perfectionism is internalised oppression.'

> 'Embrace being perfectly imperfect. Learn from your mistakes and forgive yourself; you'll be happier.'
>
> **ROY BENNETT**

3.4 Learn to listen

> 'We have two ears and one mouth, so we should listen more than we say.' **ZENO OF CITIUM, GREEK PHILOSOPHER**

We've all heard the compliment 'He is a great listener'. True, listening is one of the most important skills you can develop in building your career and nurturing your relationships, and yet for most folk, it doesn't come naturally. The problem is that we all listen from our own point of view, our own upbringing, our own position. In his famous book, *The 7 Habits of Highly Effective People*[21], Steven Covey wrote: 'Most of us don't listen with the intent to understand. We listen with the intent to reply.'

The starting point of becoming a great listener is to be curious, to start every conversation with the belief that you have something to learn.

I'm sure you've been annoyed by the person who, one you start chatting, immediately shares their experience. If you are telling them about your difficult partner, they interrupt to go one up with their relationship dramas. If you've got a problem at work, they have a boss who is a catastrophe. A good listener doesn't equate their experience. If someone is talking about having lost a family member, don't start talking about the time you had a death in your family. No two experiences are the same and the conversation shouldn't be about you. The spiritual teacher Ram Dass said: 'The quieter you become, the more you can hear.'

Simone Weil was a French philosopher, writer and activist, and I find two of her quotes especially moving. Simone tells us that listening is an act of love. 'Attention is the rarest and purest form of generosity', and 'The love of our neighbour in all its fullness simply means being able to ask what are you going through?'

Marion's story:
'I'm a social worker at a hospital and normally I rely on body language and facial expressions to get a feel for what people are really saying, but during Covid, with patients wearing masks and hospital staff clad in PPE, that was no longer possible. I had to hone my listening skills, to listen with all my concentration. And that's been a gift'.

> 'ATTENTION IS THE RAREST AND PUREST FORM OF GENEROSITY'.

When we are listening, we need to be fully present and focused on the conversation. Humble inquiry[22] is the fine art of drawing someone out, of asking questions to which you don't already know the answer, of building a relationship based on curiosity and interest in the other person. Humble inquiry questions are the opposite of leading questions where you're trying to get the other person to confirm what you already believe or are thinking.

When it comes to the workplace, one of the leading management thinkers in the world, Prof Roger Martin,[23] says: 'A great leader's first reaction is: "Hmm, say more. Tell me more ...", because it has this super big knock-on effect. It causes all your subordinates to think that if you've got an interesting thought, I'm open to hearing it. I'm not going to just shut that down because I disagree with it. Everybody is more inclined to think about things and think about things differently, and not be afraid of that.'

How to be a good listener at work

- Ask questions that are as open-ended as possible.
- Start with questions around the basics – who, where, when, what, how.
- Move on to questions like: 'What's going on?' 'How did you feel?' 'What was the impact? 'Can you give me an example?'
- These types of questions avoid yes or no answers and carry no judgement.
- Think about the difference between 'What did you do?' and 'Why didn't you do something?'
- If someone is going through hell, just listen and tell them you're with them. That's what they need – support, not advice. (This approach will build your personal relationships too.)

If you watch top business people at a meeting, you'll see that winners aren't interested in proving how much they know. They are interested in getting as much information as possible from the others in the room. If someone says something they disagree with, they don't try and prove them wrong; they ask questions and listen to the answers so that they can better understand and then get to the correct answer.

When there is conflict, the best thing you can do in a difficult conversation is to listen. Everyone wants to be heard, especially when there are problems and emotions are bubbling over. If you ask questions in a non-threatening and unbiased way, you are acknowledging the other person. It doesn't really matter whether you agree or not and whether the opinions voiced have merit or not – just listening to everyone will defuse the situation.

> 'Being heard is so close to being loved that, for the average person, they are almost indistinguishable.' **DAVID W. AUGSBURGER**

3.5 Communicate

> 'The art of communication is the language of leadership.' **JAMES HUMES**

Communicating well is a great confidence builder. Some people are naturally good at communicating and others find it difficult. It is something we can all learn though, and good communication skills are a huge asset in your relationships at home and at work.

The first step in effective communications is to become an engaged listener (see 3.4). Do less talking and more listening. And listening isn't only about understanding what is being said but also the emotions behind the words. It's often the subtle intonations that convey the real message. If you want to coach your team at work, active listening is where you should start.

Here are other skills we all need to become good communicators:

* Be honest and sincere.
* Pay attention to non-verbal signals. Your body language, which includes facial expressions, eye contact, nodding, your posture, and the

tone of your voice, can help you connect with others. A simple head nod or smile can encourage team members to feel heard. (Bear in mind that people from different countries and cultures tend to use different non-verbal gestures.)

* Watch your audience for signs that they are not engaging or aligning themselves with you. Ideally, they should be nodding and making eye contact. If not, you may need to change your style.
* Stay calm under pressure. Use stalling tactics like asking for something to be repeated, while you give yourself time to think. Take time to answer.
* Look for humour in any situation.
* Be specific and clear, especially when you are communicating at work. The clearer you are, the less confusion there will be around priorities.
* At work, let people see you. Don't only rely on emails and company WhatsApps – have some face-to-face chats. Ask for feedback and act on it.
* As a leader, be transparent in sharing the company's goals and challenges.

... GOOD COMMUNICATION SKILLS ARE A HUGE ASSET IN YOUR RELATIONSHIPS AT HOME AND AT WORK.

You may have to communicate your project or ideas at short notice without a prepared PowerPoint and you will need to be understood and convincing. Matt Abrahams, a lecturer in organisational behaviour at Stanford Graduate School of Business, has developed a great framework for pitching ideas and concepts[24]. This structure has only four simple sentences:

'***What if you could …***' paints a picture of what is possible through your product, service, or idea, e.g. 'What if we had a top-quality coffee machine in our office …'

'***So that …***' connects to a meaningful, relevant goal for the listener, e.g. '… so that employees don't feel the need to go out when they want a coffee?'

'***For example …***' makes things concrete and demonstrates existing traction, e.g. 'At the moment people are taking 20 minutes to go out whenever they want a coffee and that's not good for productivity.'

'***And that's not all …***' demonstrates potential, additional future opportunities, e.g. 'We could charge the cost to team building, and once a week we could have an informal coffee meeting with all the staff to exchange ideas and updates.'

So: no waffling, no um-ing and ah-ing – a simple clear, concise framework. Try it!

> 'The most important thing in communication is to hear what isn't being said.' **PETER DRUKER**

3.6 Just breathe

> 'There is a me that I could be. If I just let her breathe outside. A thundering song that I could sing. If I just let her breathe outside.' **LEBO MASHILE**

Breathing is one of the simplest and most effective ways of managing stress, anxiety and general feelings of uptightness. We don't think about breathing – we take in about 23,000 breaths a day and never give it a thought. But when we are stressed or anxious, our body responds as it did when we were living in caves and always on guard – our breath gets shallower and faster in order to send more oxygen to our muscles so that we can run faster and fight better.

That's really not helpful for modern living, and so we need to use our breathing to calm ourselves and send messages to our body that we are safe. Conscious slow breathing through the nose, deep into our diaphragm, activates the 'rest and digest' parasympathetic nervous system that is the very opposite of 'fight and flight'. I promise you that when you are nervous about a presentation or facing a deadline or going on a date or sitting in traffic worrying about being late, **a few slow, deep breaths are all you need to feel calm and in control**.

Modern science suggests that the best and fastest way to reduce stress is to use what is called the 'physiological sigh'. You take two consecutive breaths, back to back, breathing in as deeply as you can through your nose and filling your lungs to the maximum and then exhaling fully to completely empty your lungs. It's really simple, works immediately and you can do it anywhere.

The spiritual teacher Eckhart Tolle says: 'Being aware of your breath forces you into the present moment – the key to all inner transformation. Whenever you are conscious of the breath, you are absolutely present. You may notice that you cannot think and be aware of your breathing. Conscious breathing stops your mind.'

When I'm anxious, I practise four-square breathing:

- ☺ Breathe in for four slow counts up the side of an imaginary square
- ☺ Hold at the top of the square for four slow counts
- ☺ Exhale down the other side for four counts
- ☺ Hold along the bottom for the last four
- ☺ Repeat
- ☺ A couple of rounds of that and nothing will faze you.

There are lots of other breathing patterns – you can breathe in through the nose for four, hold the breath for two, and then breathe out for six, saying 'relax' under your breath as you exhale.

A yoga breathing technique known as the 'relaxing breath' involves breathing in for four seconds, holding the breath for seven seconds, and exhaling for eight seconds – this one is especially good for helping you to fall asleep.

You can even practise breathing while you walk – always through your nose, breathe in for five steps and out for five steps. Find a pattern that works for you and practise it a few times a day. You'll feel so much less anxious generally and you'll have the skill at your fingertips when you suddenly feel overwhelmed.

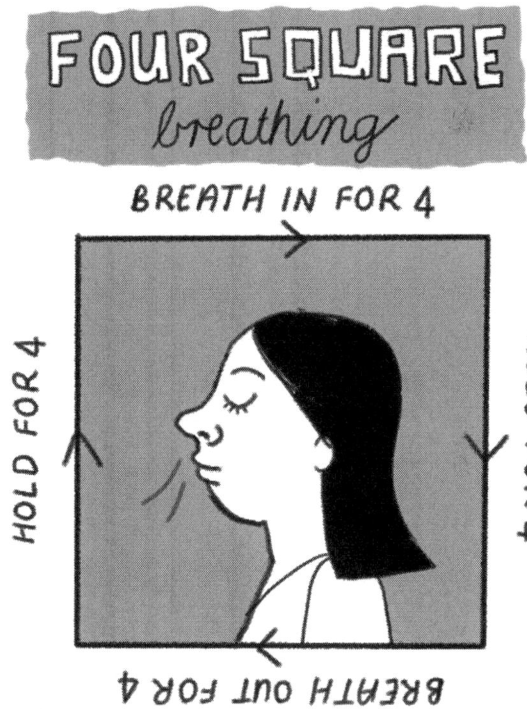

> 'When you arise in the morning, think of what a precious privilege it is to be alive, to breathe, to think, to enjoy, to love.' **MARCUS AURELIUS**

3.7 Stand up for yourself

> 'When our body language is confident and open, other people respond in kind, unconsciously reinforcing not only their perception of us but also our perception of ourselves.' **AMY CUDDY**

Physical poses can increase your power. It matters how you stand and how you sit. In a study conducted by professors from Columbia and Harvard, students who posed in high-power non-verbal displays experienced a rise in testosterone, decreases in cortisol, had increased feelings of power and a greater tolerance for risk, while those posing in low-power poses had the opposite.[25] The high-power poses were standing up straight and taking up space or standing up to lean across over a table towards someone, while low-power poses were seated, hunched up, arms folded, looking down.

In a different study, researchers at Ohio State University found that people who were told to sit up straight and write down why they were qualified for a job were more likely to believe their thoughts about their qualifications than those who wrote while slumped over their desk[26]. So, it seems that posture affects how you think about yourself. **If you sit up straight, you will be more confident of your abilities** – something to remember for your next Zoom meeting!

Oscar-winning actress Helen Mirren tells this story: 'Fresh from a costume fitting, where I had been posing in front of the mirror assuming what I thought was a strong position – arms folded, butch-looking ... you know – I met with the woman in charge of Holloway police station. She gave me the most invaluable advice: "Never let them see you cry, and never cross your arms." When I asked why, she said "because it is a defensive action and therefore weak."'

When you walk tall, sit up straight and look confident, your brain reflects that confidence in your thinking. Standing up straight activates the sympathetic nervous system, which is associated with feelings of excitement and energy. It doesn't matter whether you really are confident – your body language says you are and that makes you powerful.

> WHEN YOU WALK TALL, SIT UP STRAIGHT AND LOOK CONFIDENT, YOUR BRAIN REFLECTS THAT CONFIDENCE IN YOUR THINKING.

Being your power

- When you join a meeting, don't tuck yourself in at the end of the table; rather sit down in the middle.
- Enter with a smile for everyone – smiling suggest you are relaxed and in charge.
- Don't volunteer to take the notes – only do it if asked.
- Don't volunteer to pour the tea.
- Don't end your suggestions asking for affirmation with words like 'Right?' or 'At least that's what I think'.
- Finish what you want to say and don't let anyone interrupt you.
- If you are interrupted, pick up the conversation again or ask the person to let you finish.

> 'Confidence is everything, and the way you carry yourself, your posture, eye contact, all of that is such a big role in impressions, regardless of your size.' **CAMILLE KOSTEK, MODEL**

3.8 Play to your strengths

> 'Don't push your weaknesses, play with your strengths.' **JENNIFER LOPEZ**

I'm not a huge fan of personality tests that tell you you're an introvert, or a type A personality or, in Enneagram language, a Loyal Sceptic or an Active Controller. It can be useful in the workplace to have insights into people's personalities, but once you have a label, what do you do with it? As tennis supremo Martina Navratilova once said: 'Labels are for filing. Labels are for clothing. Labels are not for people.'

What I do think is very helpful is to find out what your strengths are. Character strengths are the positive parts of your personality that make you feel authentic and engaged. Research has shown that understanding and using your strengths will help you boost your confidence, increase your happiness, strengthen your relationships and manage problems.

Professor Martin Seligman, Director of the Positive Psychology Center at UCLA, studied personality traits, virtues, strengths and weaknesses all over the world and in different cultures and developed a universal list of 24 character strengths that apply to anyone in any country. Together with Dr Neal Mayerson, he created Values In Action (VIA), now known as the VIA Institute on Character, which identifies these character strengths that all people have in varying degrees. You can identify your own strengths by going to www.viacharacter.org and taking their free survey. According to the website, over 15 million people have done it. It's so worth-while because often people aren't aware of their best qualities.

The 24 strengths © have been grouped as follows:

1. **WISDOM**

   - **Creativity:** Thinking of new ways to do things
   - **Curiosity:** Taking an interest in a wide variety of topics
   - **Open-mindedness:** Examining things from all sides; thinking things through
   - **Love of Learning:** Mastering new topics, skills, and bodies of research
   - **Perspective:** Being able to provide wise counsel to others; looking at the world in a way that makes sense

2. **COURAGE**

- **Honesty:** Speaking the truth; being authentic and genuine
- **Bravery:** Embracing challenges, difficulties, or pain; not shrinking from threat
- **Persistence:** Finishing things once they are started
- **Zest:** Approaching all things in life with energy and excitement

3. **HUMANITY (LOVE)**

- **Kindness:** Doing favours and good deeds
- **Love:** Valuing close relationships with others
- **Social Intelligence:** Being aware of other people's motives and feelings

4. **JUSTICE**

- **Fairness:** Treating all people the same
- **Leadership:** Organising group activities and making sure they happen
- **Teamwork:** Working well with others as a group or a team

5. TEMPERANCE

- **Forgiveness:** Forgiving others who have wronged them
- **Modesty:** Letting one's successes and accomplishments stand on their own
- **Prudence:** Avoiding doing things they might regret; making good choices
- **Self-regulation:** Being disciplined; controlling one's appetites and emotions

6. TRANSCENDENCE

- **Appreciation of Beauty:** Noticing and appreciating beauty and excellence in everything
- **Gratitude:** Being thankful for the good things; taking time to express thanks
- **Hope:** Expecting the best; working to make it happen; believing good things are possible
- **Humour:** Making other people smile or laugh; enjoying jokes
- **Religiousness:** Having a solid belief about a higher purpose and meaning of life

The survey will identify your strengths ranked from your top strengths to your lesser strengths, but there are no scores; no values are attributed to them, so even if, for example, leadership ranks low for you, it doesn't mean you can't be a leader. When you have taken the survey and seen your top strengths, you should feel 'Yes, that's right, I am like that'. The ranking is different for everyone because we are all unique.

You will be true to your authentic self when you act from your strengths. And when you use them it will feel effortless and easy. You can use your strengths at work and in your social life. Your using your strength doesn't impact negatively on anyone else.

My top three strengths are love of learning, leadership and curiosity. These have taken me on a wonderful career path across many industries and different roles. My interest in learning new things is what keeps me alive and jumping out of bed in the mornings.

> 'The meaning of life is to find your gift. The purpose of life is to give it away.' **PABLO PICASSO**

3.9 Ten ideas to think about

- You deserve self-compassion.
- You are not what happened to you, you are what you choose to become.
- Go back 10 years and realise how amazed you would be to see yourself now.
- Be grateful for what you have.
- Nature is not mute; it is man who is deaf.
- Spend your money on the things money can buy. Spend your time on the things money can't buy.
- Be a beginner every single morning.
- If you are the smartest person in the room, you're in the wrong room.
- Information is not the same as knowledge.
- You miss 100% of the shots you don't take.

3.10 Jesica's story

> 'Things happen unexpectedly, and you must roll with the moment.' **JESICA**

When Jesica Barnardo was invited to become a partner at prestigious Cape Town law firm, Von Lieres, Cooper & Barlow, she cried. It was such a huge moment in the six-year journey of an unsure girl from a poor rural community who started as a fearful candidate attorney and developed into a successful lawyer. In making partner, it was not just her dream that she had achieved, but the dream of her parents who had worked so hard for their children.

Jesica grew up as one of five siblings on a smallholding outside the little village of Kurland near Plettenberg Bay. It was a happy childhood, although her parents were very strict – at weekends her dad was a pastor in the local community church. Her parents were determined that their children should get the best education possible and encouraged them to make the most of the opportunities that they themselves had not had.

Jesica always wanted to go to university and decided early on that she would study law. She worked in her school holidays to save money, and after matriculating took a gap year, working in the tourism industry to save for her studies. She was fortunate enough to get a bursary that covered her tuition for the four years of study. Entering university with good grades and money saved up, she felt confident, but soon felt overwhelmed by the freedom and the loneliness of separation from her family. She did well academically, but her early confidence dwindled and when she graduated, she was uncertain about life outside of university. The pressure of making life-altering decisions weighed heavily and she was uncertain what her next steps should be. Her procrastination meant that she missed application deadlines and so she studied further part-time, and then went back home to work in a local hotel. She knew she would succeed in a small town and felt confident being back in familiar surroundings. However, her true passion lay in law.

Fortunately, a friend from university persuaded her to interview for a position as candidate attorney at Von Lieres in Cape Town. She got the job and started on her dream, only to find that working life was not what she had expected. Everything seemed too new and too difficult, both at work and socially. She knew the law well from her studies but it was completely different in the actual workplace. She was struggling to find her feet and continuously doubted herself. She compared herself to those around her and always found fault with how she did things. Her self-talk was all about 'I'm not meant to be here', 'I'm an imposter', 'I'm not moving forward'. Despite all her self-doubt, Von Lieres saw her potential and retained her after the completion of her articles at the end of 2016.

Jesica started to slowly build back her confidence with guidance from her boss, but she still felt reluctant to ask if she didn't know something for fear of looking 'stupid', and she wouldn't express her own ideas for fear of making mistakes. Then the company sponsored some personal coaching and the result was two life-changing insights. Jesica realised she was her own harshest critic, never acknowledging her own successes. Also, in trying to please everyone, she was undermining herself. She needed to start believing in herself and take back control of her life.

JESICA REALISED SHE WAS HER OWN HARSHEST CRITIC, NEVER ACKNOWLEDGING HER OWN SUCCESSES.

While Covid was quite devastating, it also turned out to be a positive time in Jesica's life. Working at home, independently, the realisation dawned that she was more than competent. She could be trusted to deliver. She could fix mistakes. She could learn new skills and tackle new challenges. Jesica began to push herself and to take on more work. She did not let the fear of the unknown paralyse her as it had in the past. As the office reopened, she welcomed more and more opportunities to learn, until one day her boss entrusted her with running the department independently.

Along this journey Jesica also got married and had a baby. She enthuses about life: 'Life isn't about plans, it's about living. Things happen unexpectedly, and you must roll with the moment. If you don't, you'll end up sitting in your room like I did – being miserable, endlessly overthinking. The minute you let go and welcome the fear and the changes, beautiful things happen. Things you never thought would happen.'

Jesica knows that reaching success is about confidence. She says: 'We're quick to critique ourselves but we're not conditioned to love ourselves and boost our own confidence. If you

IF YOU DON'T HAVE CONFIDENCE, YOU CAN ALWAYS BUILD IT. YOU MUST WORK ON IT. IT WON'T COME OVERNIGHT. YOU HAVE TO FEED IT, DAY IN AND DAY OUT.

don't have confidence, you can always build it. You must work on it. It won't come overnight. You have to feed it, day in and day out. Build it slowly. It's the small things that turn into big things, and what you used to struggle with becomes second nature. Take small steps, saying what you want, saying no to things and finding out that nothing ends if you take the chance.'

Jesica's favourite quote:

> 'Always dream and shoot higher than you know you can do. Don't bother just to be better than your contemporaries or predecessors. Try to be better than yourself.'
>
> **WILLIAM FAULKNER**

4.
Building your career

4.1 Harassment

> 'The fact that women begin to avoid running for public office because of the harassment, and sometimes even violence, that they face as a hazard means that the world is being robbed of extraordinary leadership that women can bring to bear.'
>
> **PHUMZILE MLAMBO-NGCUKA**

Harassment of any kind is a total no-no, and don't ever allow it to undermine you and your confidence. Your dignity has value.

When I started working, sexual harassment was so commonplace that I took it for granted, tried to ignore it and handled it as best I could. Women were always paid less than men. Males were always commenting on what women wore, asking them out, undermining them at meetings. I remember one director, a big ugly man, would never call me by my name but always called me 'meisie' (Afrikaans for little girl). Thank goodness for the #MeToo movement and for today's more enlightened attitudes around what constitutes sexual harassment.

There are many forms of harassment. It's not limited to the sexual, but can also be about religious beliefs, race, country of origin and sexual orientation. As far as I am concerned, discrimination is another evil form of harassment. Derogatory remarks or jokes about headscarves and terrorists, skin colour and accent, and LGBTQ lifestyles are still commonplace in many workplaces, especially around young workers.

HARASSMENT OF ANY KIND IS A TOTAL NO-NO, AND DON'T EVER ALLOW IT TO UNDERMINE YOU AND YOUR CONFIDENCE.

Don't stand for it.

- Use your FU power (see 2.11).
- Make it clear that these comments are unwelcome, that the person's behavior offends you. Do not ignore it and hope it will go away.
- Don't try to deflect it by flirting.
- Pretend you don't get the innuendo or the double entendre; look the offender in the eye and stare him or her down. Ask him or her to repeat what they just said – that usually shames people into silence.
- Stand up for your colleagues if they are being pestered.
- Always refuse invitations outside of work.
- Avoid flings at work – colleagues will spread rumours that you have used sex to get ahead or they'll mistrust you because you have an inside track.

Harassment and prejudice around race is a tougher problem in polarised societies, which is where the world seems to be heading. But that's all the more reason that it should be addressed. Martin Luther King said that our lives begin to end the day we become silent about things that

MARTIN LUTHER KING SAID THAT OUR LIVES BEGIN TO END THE DAY WE BECOME SILENT ABOUT THINGS THAT MATTER.

matter. Keep a record of any demeaning remarks, document any incidents, talk to your colleagues and see if they will support you in a formal complaint to your company. The downside is that there can be a problem with formal complaints because there can be retaliation in some form or another – you may get ostracised or transferred or overlooked for promotion. It is illegal to discriminate in most countries, so seeing a lawyer or going to the labour court is a potential option. Otherwise, move on to another department or even another company if you can.

> 'And then there is the kindness of dignity. Of giving someone the benefit of the doubt. The kindness of seeing someone for the person that they are and can become, and the realisation that everyone, including me and you, has a noise in our heads, a story to be told, fear to be danced with and dreams to be realised.' **SETH GODIN**

4.2 Smashing the interview

> 'Whether you think you can or whether you think you can't, you're right.' **HENRY FORD**

Sooner or later you are going to have that all-important interview. It might be for your first job or it might be for a new job that you really want. Whatever the case, you'll need to feel as confident as you can, and the good news is that there is a technique that can help you be successful.

First, a quick run through the basics:

- Make sure your online presence is up to date and you have a good photograph of yourself on all your profiles.
- Dress neatly and conservatively and be early.
- Have positive non-verbal communication – firm handshake, look people in the eye, sit up straight, look interested, smile.
- Listen before you talk and give careful answers – don't babble or be long-winded no matter how nervous you are.
- Do your research on the company beforehand so that you can answer and ask questions about it.
- Be positive about your achievements but be real and not arrogant.
- Prepare answers to possible questions. You'll find lists of common questions on the internet, like: 'Where do you see yourself in five years?' 'Why do you want to work here?' 'What is your greatest achievement outside of work?' 'How would your direct reports describe you?'

- Be prepared to give examples of times when you have solved a problem relevant to the job you're going to be doing, like: 'Give me an example of how you have handled a setback/missed a deadline/dealt with an aggressive customer.'
- Ask if there is anything else you can provide, like references or work samples.
- Thank the interviewer for his or her time.
- After the interview, send a thank you note, handwritten if possible.

And now for the technique. It is called WOOP[27] and was developed by academic and psychologist Prof Gabriele Oettingen. To quote from the WOOP website: 'Based on 20 years of research in the science of motivation, WOOP presents a unique and surprising idea – the obstacles that we think most prevent us from fulfilling our wishes can actually help us to realise them.'

... THE OBSTACLES THAT WE THINK MOST PREVENT US FROM FULFILLING OUR WISHES CAN ACTUALLY HELP US TO REALISE THEM.

WOOP is a scientifically proven tool that can help you achieve your goals. It uses a form of visualisation called mental contrasting, and stands for **W**ish, **O**utcome, **O**bstacle, and **P**lan.

Here's how it works:

You sit quietly and focus on answering these questions.

1. **Wish**: What is it you want to achieve (you need to specify a time frame)? So, for an interview it would be 'to have a successful interview tomorrow'.
2. **Outcome:** What would be the best thing, the best outcome about fulfilling your wish? How would fulfilling your wish make you feel? The answer could be 'I will get the job I so badly want. I will be overjoyed because I will have a better salary and I know I am going to be happy working there. I'll be able to help my family too.'
3. **Obstacle:** What is it in within you that holds you back from fulfilling your wish? What stands in the way? What is your inner obstacle? Your answer might be 'I'm scared I'll fumble my answers,' 'I might not be able to answer the questions,' or in summary 'I feel I may not be good enough.'

4. **Plan:** Make a plan for overcoming your obstacle. What action would help you when your obstacle shows up? Create an if/then plan and visualise it in your mind.

   '**If/When** I feel I am not good enough, **then** I will tell myself that I can do this.' **'If/When** I feel I'm not good enough, **then** I will reassure myself that I am qualified and experienced.' '**If/When** I fumble my answers, **then** I'll apologise and ask if I can repeat the answer.' And so on. Think of an **if/then** scenario for as many obstacles as you can visualise.

You can use WOOP for any kind of goal, big or small, like losing weight, going to the gym, finishing a work project, making a good presentation or having a successful meeting. There's even a free app that you can download. It seems so simple but you'll be surprised how well it works.

> 'You are enough just as you are'.
> **MEGHAN MARKLE**

4.3 Reframe

> 'We can't solve problems by using the same kind of thinking we used when we created them.' **ALBERT EINSTEIN**

Imagine you are to present to a new, powerful client. You've put in a lot of work but you are so nervous that you are convinced you will dry up and make a fool of yourself and will never make a sale. If you reframe the appointment as the chance to meet this client and learn from them what their needs are so that you can then come back to them with a tailor-made product, you will be way less nervous. If possible, try to see sales meetings as potentially exciting collaborations and you will be surprised at the positive results.

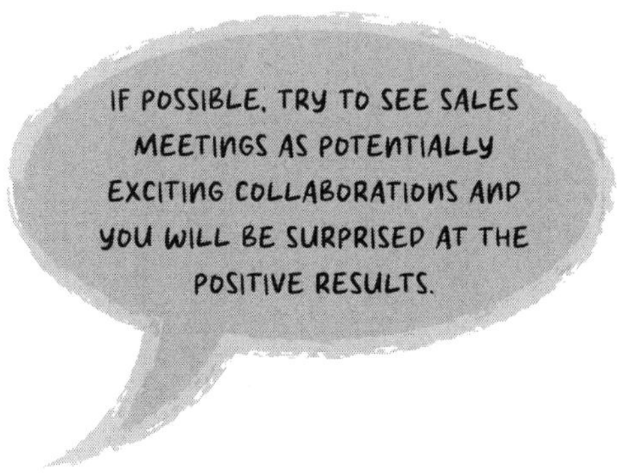

Imagine you have just submitted a proposal that you have worked hard on. When you get a note from your boss (whom you dislike) saying that she would like to chat to you about your proposal as she has some suggestions, how do you feel about that meeting? If that same note came from a boss you like and admire, how you would feel about the meeting? What would your body language and attitude be like in the two different meetings?

Situations are neutral – we give them meaning and each person will have a different response to the same situation. One person may be over the moon that she got promoted while another may be terrified that she won't be good enough to deliver.

Through reframing, we can challenge the 'frame' – the underlying assumptions and interpretations we have made about different situations. There's a great saying: 'When you change the way you look at things, the things you look at change.'

Reframing is a powerful way to cope with challenges and setbacks when our negative thinking is at its worst. If you are thinking 'this happened because I am not good enough', you will never achieve your potential. Ask yourself: 'On what have I based this limiting belief? Is it true?

Can I learn something worthwhile from what's happened?'

Here are some examples of reframing your thinking.

- 'Anyone can do what I do.' REFRAME as 'I am unique and they want me to do it my way.'
- 'I can't handle this.' REFRAME as 'This is a tough challenge. I'll do what I can and if necessary, I'll ask for help. But I can see I'm going to learn a lot doing it.'
- 'I always get things wrong.' REFRAME as 'Everyone gets stuff wrong some time and I have got some important things right in the past.'
- 'This Tinder date will be a disaster.' REFRAME as 'I can enjoy myself even if the date is ghastly – at the very least I'll have a story to tell my friends.'
- 'This is all my fault.' REFRAME as 'I accept that I contributed to the problem, but so many outside factors made it worse that I can't blame myself for everything.'

- 'My to-do list is insane. I'll never get through it.' REFRAME as 'If I tackle this one bit at a time, I'll get through it by the end of the week.'
- 'I won't ever get over my ex.' REFRAME as 'It was for the best that we broke up now rather than later. I won't feel this bad a few months down the line. I will find someone else special.'

We can apply reframing in so many areas.

> If you don't like something, change it; if you can't change it, change the way you think about it.' **MARY ENGELBREIT**

4.4 Imposter syndrome

> 'When you undervalue what you do, the world will undervalue who you are.' **OPRAH WINFREY**

I'm sure there isn't a person anywhere who hasn't at some stage thought: 'I shouldn't be here. I don't belong here with all these clever people. They're going to find out I don't know what I'm doing'. Feeling like a fraud is common, and for some people it is almost impossible to shake it off, no matter the situation. The psychologists have named this the 'imposter syndrome' and I have seen so many people, especially women, battle with it. If you are always thinking that you're a fraud and likely to fail, you should know that you aren't alone.

Psychologist Pauline Rose Clance[28] first identified imposter syndrome in 1978. Here's what she writes about those who have it: 'Even though they are often very successful by external standards, they feel their success has been due to some mysterious fluke or luck or great effort; they are afraid their achievements are due to "breaks" and not the result of their own ability and competence. They are also pretty certain that, unless they go to gargantuan efforts to do so, success can't be repeated. They are afraid that "next time, I will blow it."' Her research found that imposter syndrome is present in all genders, races, ages and occupations but it is more prevalent in disadvantaged or underrepresented groups and seems to affect them more.

Here's what Valerie Young, who wrote a book on imposter syndrome, says: 'People who don't feel like impostors are no more intelligent or capable or talented or qualified than those who do. The only difference between them and us is that in the exact situation that triggers an impostor response in us … they are thinking different thoughts. That's it.'[29]

And here's what Adam Grant, professor of psychology at the Wharton School of the University of Pennsylvania, has to say: 'Impostor syndrome is not a sign that other people are overestimating you. It's more likely that you're underestimating your potential. Confidence is often a consequence of growth, not a cause. Believing in your ability is less important than believing in your ability to improve.'

What can you do about imposter syndrome?

- As with most problems, the best way to deal with imposter syndrome is to talk about it.
- Open up to your colleagues and friends for support. You'll find many of them, even the most senior and experienced, feel or have felt the same way that you do.
- It's important to acknowledge your successes and stop undervaluing yourself.
- Recognise your own competence. If someone else thinks you can do the job, never doubt yourself.
- Remember you are in your position because someone thought you had the talent or skills to be there.
- Remind yourself every day that you belong.

> 'I have written eleven books but each time I think "uh-oh they're going to find out now. I've run a game on everybody and they're going to find me out."' **MAYA ANGELOU**

4.5 Don't be small – you're not

> 'There is no passion to be found playing small – in settling for a life that is less than the one you are capable of living.' **NELSON MANDELA**

Prominent Human Rights lawyer, Faranaaz Veriava, was asked in a newspaper interview in 2020: 'What thing do you wish you had learnt earlier in your life?' and her answer was: 'I was submissive for too long. As a young black female advocate at the Johannesburg Bar, I tolerated intimidation and exclusion and I allowed it to make me small: I wish I had come into my own confidence and power sooner.'

Women are often guilty of playing small. We are conditioned to be agreeable, not to make a fuss, to be the peacemakers, but this comes at a personal cost. It is hard to be true to yourself if you are backing down, keeping quiet or not sharing your views. Women in business are often scared to be assertive for fear of being labelled a bitch or boastful, while men are admired for defending their views and being competitive.

People who don't know how to be assertive can end up being bullied at work, or getting underpaid because they don't ask for a raise. They end up with all the shitty jobs because they don't know how to say no. Rather than being miserable and resigning yourself to not being heard, take responsibility and assert yourself.

If you are asked to do something that you know for some reason you can't manage, don't delay replying because you feel guilty or want to be nice or don't want to disappoint people. A quick 'No, I'm sorry, I can't manage that' is much better than leaving people hanging for an answer or thinking you will be handling the request and then letting them down.

WOMEN ARE OFTEN GUILTY OF PLAYING SMALL. WE ARE CONDITIONED TO BE AGREEABLE, NOT TO MAKE A FUSS, TO BE THE PEACEMAKERS, BUT THIS COMES AT A PERSONAL COST.

There are ways to be assertive without being obnoxious.

- Make eye contact.
- Don't ever apologise for wanting to be treated fairly.
- Ask directly and clearly for whatever it is you want – don't assume that people know because often they don't.
- Set clear boundaries in every aspect of your life.
- However, don't insist on being right – listen respectfully to different ideas or arguments and keep an open mind to other points of view.
- In disagreements, look for common ground.

When you are passionate about something and you are blocked, don't complain or attack even if you know that you are in the right. Try to persuade and motivate people to change. We can all be inspired by the example of Greta Thunberg, the Swedish teenager who has ignited a global movement for climate change. She is always totally authentic, driven not by a desire for fame or money, but by her total conviction that the world must act on global warming.

Own your achievements. Give yourself credit for how far you have come – that's the way to feel confident to tackle even bigger challenges in the future. As TV personality Mel Robbins says: 'There will always be someone who can't see your worth. Don't let it be you.'

This what the actor Denzel Washington tweeted about valuing yourself: 'If I do a job in 30 minutes, it is because I spent 10 years learning and progressing on how to do that in 30 minutes. I base what is owed to me on the years, not the minutes.'

A friend of mine shared this story about women standing up for themselves. 'My sister was CEO of a property development body; she went to an international conference. Because she was the only woman at her level, the organisers sat her at the table with the event managers and marketers, so she could be with "the girls". But they were all extremely junior and it meant she was excluded from the power table. Being my sister, she kicked up a fuss and insisted on being seated with her peers, and then she was "the bitch".'

When you stand up for yourself and don't back down, people will call you names. I've been called a mad woman, a cow, a bitch and worse. There are people who can't handle strong women (hopefully that is changing) and there are far too many unhappy trolls who bolster their own miserable self-worth by attacking others. This is not your problem – it's theirs. Let it be. Ignore it.

> 'You are a child of God. Your playing small does not serve the world. There is nothing enlightened about shrinking so that other people won't feel insecure around you. We are all meant to shine as children do. We were born to make manifest the glory of God that is within us. It is not just in some of us; it's in everyone. And as we let our own light shine, we unconsciously give other people permission to do the same. As we are liberated from our own fear, our presence automatically liberates others.' **MARIANNE WILLIAMSON**

4.6 What is your brand?

> 'Why fit in when you were born to stand out?' **DR. SEUSS**

One of the routes to greater confidence is the recognition that you yourself are a brand – something like a soap or a toothpaste but a person version. For a brand to be successful, it needs to be trusted, and in building your personal brand you need to tap into your integrity and your authentic self as the place to begin. We have to decide what it is we want to be known for, what we want people to be saying about us after we have left the room.

The starting point is with your values and how you live them, so you need to be clear on those. You can't build a credible brand without being authentic. If you answered the questions in 2.3, you'll have a good idea of the authentic you. Now you can go further and ask: 'What do I do really well?' 'What is my goal here?' 'What can I offer the world?' 'Which of my values do I want to promote?'

A positive way to answer these questions is to write a personal brand image statement – a few sentences about how you would describe yourself and how you want to impact others. Try to sum up the best and most interesting parts of yourself.

Social media exposes us quite ruthlessly. We can enhance our brand or ruin our brand with one simple post. Employers check out the social media of prospective employees, and drunken parties and inappropriate comments may mean the end of someone's job prospects. Always think twice before you post. But, on the positive side, being online gives you the opportunity to be more visible, more accessible and to stand out. Your social media should reflect the brand image you want to portray.

Think of building your brand as giving yourself a competitive edge in building your career. Here are some ideas on how to go about it:

- Be on every one of the important social media platforms.
- Position yourself as a thought leader by posting articles by experts or news about your industry or profession and, best of all, by writing your own original material (preferably not AI generated!).

> **YOU CAN'T BUILD A CREDIBLE BRAND WITHOUT BEING AUTHENTIC.**

- When you are posting, take the time to check your spelling and grammar.
- If you can, find something unique or different about yourself; however simple, it will help people remember you.
- When your company is making videos, volunteer to take part – not to be the star but just to contribute. It will get you noticed.
- Do some voluntary work in an area that you value. It will enrich you personally and build your worth in other people's eyes.
- Be proactive at work. Ask colleagues if you can help them.
- Build trust with your co-workers, and your boss will notice.
- Be the person who always says thank you.

> 'What makes you different or weird – that's your strength.' **MERYL STREEP**

4.7 Put up your hand – the art of self-promotion

> 'Self-promotion is a leadership and political skill that is critical to master in order to navigate the realities of the workplace and position you for success.' **BONNIE MARCUS**

I grew up with Calvinist parents who, although not particularly religious, were big into humility. As children, we were taught never to boast and got very little praise for any of our accomplishments in case we got 'swollen-headed'. As a result, I've always been a 'put your head down and deliver' and 'let your results speak for you' person.

The trouble is that in today's competitive, noisy world, your results often don't speak loudly enough for you to be heard. No one is going to know what you have done unless you tell them.

People who promote themselves are more likely to land a job, more likely to build better networks and go on to be successful. Self-promotion is particularly challenging for women and many struggle with it throughout their career. We all agree the world needs smart, diverse people sharing their knowledge and opinions and it serves no one if we feel we can't put up our hands. Once you know what your personal brand is (see 4.6), you need to get out there and market it.

The starting point is to believe in your accomplishments. As an example, never think that you were invited to speak at a conference, be on a panel or attend an event simply because they needed a woman or a person of colour on the agenda. There's nothing wrong with being proud of doing something well, of your wins. Tell people what you are excited about.

> WE ALL AGREE THE WORLD NEEDS SMART, DIVERSE PEOPLE SHARING THEIR KNOWLEDGE AND OPINIONS AND IT SERVES NO ONE IF WE FEEL WE CAN'T PUT UP OUR HANDS.

Keep a score sheet of your successes, big and small, and practise sharing them by stating them as facts, clearly and without exaggeration. This is very important at work if you are asking for a raise or applying for a promotion. Don't assume your boss knows. Be unapologetic in quietly setting out your worth. In her best-selling book *Brag Better*,[30] Meredith Fineman suggests that you need to be proud, loud (and by that she means consistent messaging, repeated often) and strategic (you need to know what you want).

In a meeting, ask yourself: 'What do I know that they don't?' Remember, only you can do what you can do, the way that you can do it. Never apologise for what you don't know; rather invite people to fill you in. Use words that convey confidence, like 'I've got a good idea' or 'I can add something here' or 'What about?' rather than 'I think' 'I hope' 'I suppose'.

Social media has made us very aware of loud 'bragging' and fearful that others may criticise us for just that. As we saw in not playing small, that is their issue, not yours. And you can be grateful and generous in your promoting yourself – thankful for what you have achieved and determined to also uplift your quieter colleagues by doing their bragging for them.

> 'People don't get promoted for doing their jobs really well. They get promoted by demonstrating their potential to do more.' **TARA JAYE FRANK**

4.8 Scoring goals

> 'I don't focus on what I'm up against. I focus on my goals and I try to ignore the rest.' **VENUS WILLIAMS**

A while back it was fashionable for corporates to talk about BHGs – Big Hairy Goals. Goals are important because you need to have some idea of what you are aiming for in life, but they don't have to be huge and they don't need to be hairy.

I love the question: 'How do you eat an elephant?' and the answer: 'One bite a time' because it is great advice for most goals. If your goal is a big one like getting your degree, focus on one subject at a time, one year at a time. If you create smaller goals, the chances are you won't feel overwhelmed. Procrastination just feeds that elephant, making it even bigger.

Set goals that you can achieve because **small wins build confidence**. When you feel successful, even at very tiny things, it changes the way you see yourself. If you've ever been on a diet, you'll know that losing half a kilo a week keeps you confident and motivated to achieve a big weight loss goal of say 15 kilos. The same goes for training to run a half marathon. Baby steps get you there.

Setting smaller short-term goals doesn't mean you shouldn't have bold dreams for your future. A vision board is a good way to articulate your vision of what you want for yourself. A vision board is usually a big poster on to which you have stuck beautiful pictures, mementoes, inspirational quotes and affirmations that remind you of your goals. If you put the poster where you will often see it, you are bringing those goals to life and keeping the focus on the direction in which you want to be going. Vision boards are a form of visualisation and can inspire you to succeed.

Because corporates like frameworks, I've included two here that are good to know and can be useful for either your personal goals or for teams setting goals at work. The first is **GROW** and this is what it stands for:

G **Goals**: What do you really want? What area do you want to work on? What do you really want to achieve? What do you want to change?

R **Reality**: Where are you now? What isn't working? What is working? What can you do differently? What can you do better?

O **Options**: What could you do? What other ways are there? What has worked in the past?

W **Way Forward**: What will you do? When will you start?

And here's another popular tool that ensures that you set goals properly. It's a model called **SMART** and it says that goals must be:

S = Specific or significant.
M = Measurable or meaningful.
A = Attainable.
R = Relevant or rewarding.
T = Time-bound (i.e. there's a date attached).

Putting a time to goals is vital in achieving them. If you don't set a date, nothing happens. Divide your goal into smaller chunks and put a date for completion next each of them, e.g. by the end of next week I'll finish the first draft and by the end of the month I'll have a final copy.

Go for your goal, and go first. Don't wait for anyone or anything!

> 'If you don't know what you want, you'll never find it.' **RYŪ MURAKAMI**

4.9 Finding focus

> 'The successful warrior is the average man, with laser-like focus.'
>
> **BRUCE LEE**

You pick up your phone and start scrolling. Fifteen minutes later you wake up to your life and wonder how the time went by so fast. It feels as if social media casts a spell on us. And the machinery of social media is designed to do that – its algorithms feed us with stuff that keeps us engaged. The feeds we look at are designed to capture our emotional attention and they are changing the view we have of the world and stealing our ability to focus.

In today's world, we need our phones and, in many ways, they make us more productive. **But we need to distinguish between what our phones are doing for us and what they are doing to us.** There are only so many hours in a day and if we spend a big portion of them head down, looking at our phones, we won't get our work done. Some 2022 data revealed that the average American spends five hours and 24 minutes on their mobile device each day and will check their phone once every 10 to 12 minutes.[31] And there are many countries, including South Africa, where the average exceeds four hours a day. Picking your phone up can become a habit – are you picking it up only a few minutes after putting it down? And how much of that phone time is at work?

Have you ever begun a project with the best intentions, but then quickly became sidetracked and ended up not finishing what you started? That's happened to all of us, but finishing what you start is one of the wins for building confidence. If you have a report to finish, you need to be able to get all the information, understand it, analyse and write it up. You can't concentrate on what you need to do if you keep answering emails, getting bogged down in unimportant details, getting up to make coffee or checking your Twitter feed. When you're focused, you're more efficient.

Here are some ideas for improving focus:

- **Have a clear, specific goal**. If you know what you want to achieve, you can focus on that and make quick choices and decisions.
- **Learn to allocate your time.** Chunk out time slots for what you need to spend time on. In every week, you need time for yourself (eating, sleeping, exercising, watching TV,

social media, etc.). Then you need time for your relationships (partners, family, kids, friends, etc.) And finally, time for work – break that chunk into tasks (emails, meetings, phone calls, projects, reports, etc.). Try using a weekly time planner, highlighting these different chunks, rather than using a to-do list.

- **Have an uncluttered workspace.** Get rid of stuff you don't need. The only documents you should have on your desk are the ones you are working on.
- **Start by getting alert.** Becoming alert involves releasing epinephrine in the brain and body. Here's how Prof Huberman[32] suggests you go about doing that: 'One simple way to become more alert is 25–30 deep breaths (inhale through the nose, and exhale through the mouth). Then exhale your air and hold your breath with lungs empty for 15–60 seconds. Then inhale once and hold your breath. But don't force the breath hold; start to breathe normally immediately once you feel the impulse to breathe.' Another Huberman tip: 'Mental focus follows visual focus. To increase your level of focus on the task you are about to do, stare at an object or a point on a wall or screen for 30–60 seconds before starting (you can blink as needed). Then begin the task at hand.'

- When you need to focus, block interruptions. Use technology to block technology! Our smartphones can ward off calls and messages when we need to work without distractions. No pinging! Put your phone somewhere out of view so you can't peek at it.
- **Don't fool yourself into thinking you can multitask.** Research[33] has shown that even brief mental blocks created by shifting between tasks can cost as much as 40% of someone's productive time. Focus on one thing at a time.
- **Working with someone who also needs to focus can help.** There are wonderful apps and websites. Have a look at focusmate.com.
- **Take control over your work time.** Agree with your team or your boss when you can and can't be contacted out of hours and ensure that everyone sticks to the agreement.

> You don't get results by focusing on results. You get results by focusing on the actions that produce results.
>
> **MIKE HAWKINS**

4.10 Get going

> 'Life is like riding a bicycle. To keep your balance, you must keep moving.' **ALBERT EINSTEIN**

The reason Nike's slogan, 'Just do it', has been around so long is that it strikes such a strong chord with all of us who like to procrastinate, and hesitate and generally find reasons not to start. Often it is because we don't have the confidence to try.

Mel Robbins is an American TV host and motivational speaker who wrote a book, *The 5 Second Rule*[34]. Her belief is that if you are thinking about acting on a goal, you must physically move within five seconds or your brain will kill the idea. She writes: 'The moment you feel an instinct or a desire to action a goal or a commitment, use the rule. When you feel yourself hesitate before doing something that you know you should, count down 5-4-3-2-1-GO and move towards action.' Because our brain always tries to protect us, when it senses we are hesitant or anxious, it tries to stop us by generating doubting thoughts. A conscious decision to count down 5-4-3-2-1-GO-Action

activates the prefrontal cortex, the decision-making and judgement area of the brain. This tool means no more hitting the snooze button when you should be getting up to go to the gym. No more answering another email rather than starting that report. No more scrolling when you should be getting dinner ready.

Why not have your own CEO meeting? An important action step is to start your week with your own CEO meeting. You are the person in charge of yourself so think of yourself as your own CEO and ask yourself: 'What am I going to achieve this week?' 'What will I spend the most time on?' 'What decisions do I need to make?' 'What work needs to be completed?' 'What am I going to do to make sure my relationships are flourishing?' 'How will I grow as a person this week?'

This matrix, first developed by Stephen Covey in his book *The 7 Habits of Highly Effective People*[35], can help you tackle a week that looks overwhelming. Start with what is urgent and important, and don't neglect important and not

urgent. Try to manage interruptions like emails and phone calls and ignore distractions like social media and office gossip.

Quick wins are super important for building confidence, and another useful way of approaching work is to use the Action Priority Matrix. Here you look at the effort versus the impact to decide what you should be focusing on. Identify the quick wins and complete as many as you can. Think about how to manage your time more effectively when it comes to the major projects. See if you can delegate some of the fill-in tasks, and drop those hard slogs – you'll get stuck there and they are usually thankless.

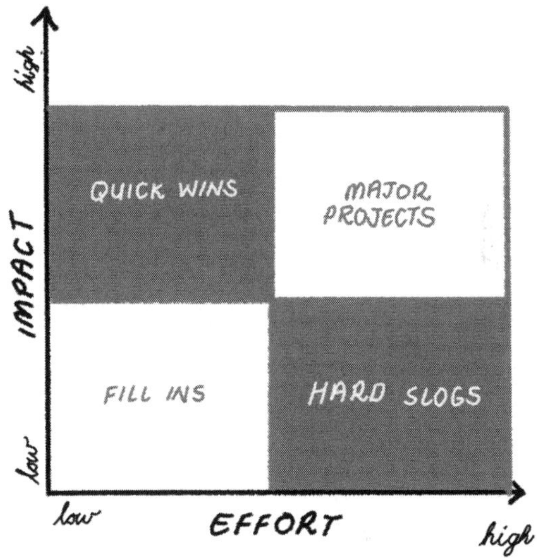

If you are determined to reach a goal, you will think of everything you need to do to achieve it, but sometimes you don't stop to question whether you will have to give up something or do less of something to achieve it.

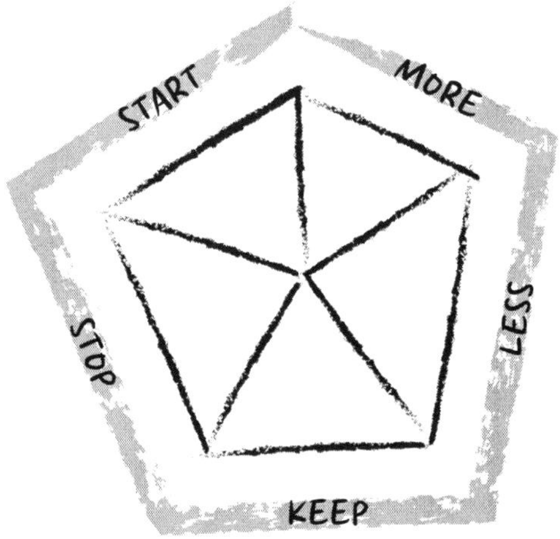

So, filling in this little pentagram can be a useful reality check. 'What will you need to start doing?' 'What do you need to do less of?' 'What do you need to stop?'

One more tip – a public declaration of what you are going to do, like 'I'm starting my own business' or 'I'm going to run a half marathon', will definitely help get you going. You are much less likely to stop at the first hurdle if you have told other people, especially those who count in your life, what you have planned.

> 'Do the best you can until you know better. Then when you know better, do better.' **MAYA ANGELOU**

4.11 When it's your turn to present

> 'You are not being judged; the value of what you are bringing to the audience is being judged.' **SETH GODIN**

All of us will have to make a speech at some time, whether it's a family gathering, a work event or a formal business presentation. It's the ultimate confidence-draining experience for nearly everyone. Apparently 73% of the American population is terrified of public speaking – that's a higher percentage than is scared of dying, or of snakes and spiders.

The usual advice we give ourselves before public speaking is to keep calm and just breathe. But when your heart is pounding and your palms are sweating, that's easier said than done. Alison Wood Brooks, a professor at Harvard Business School, has researched a different strategy that can help. In her research[36], she found that when people decide to see their anxiety as excitement, they perform better at public speaking, at maths tests and even at karaoke singing. Brooks called

I AM EXCITED.
I AM EXCITED.
I AM EXCITED.

this reappraising, and doing this can be as simple as saying out loud 'I am excited' several times, or ordering yourself to 'get excited', either of which switches your brain from a high-arousal anxiety state to a high-arousal state of excitement. In an excited state, you can focus on the potential positive outcomes rather than going over all the possible negative things that might happen. Decide to put energy into your presentation and a smile on your face. I know it sounds a bit simple, but I've done loads of presentations all over the world and I know it works.

P.S. Reappraising is similar to reframing, which is covered in 4.3. The difference is that reappraising refers to your internal state whereas reframing refers to how you are looking at an external situation.

> 'According to most studies, people's number one fear is public speaking. Number two is death. Death is number two! Does that sound right? That means that to the average person, if you go to a funeral, you're better off in the casket than doing the elegy.' **JERRY SEINFELD**

4.12 The courage to be creative

> 'The world is full of magic things, patiently waiting for our senses to grow sharper.' **WILLIAM BUTLER YEATS**

When we hear the word 'creativity', we immediately think of brilliant artists, musicians and writers, and for most of us our immediate reaction is 'I'm not creative. I can't even draw a straight line'. Creativity is about coming up with something new and valuable, and it's a big buzzword in business.

The reality is that we are all capable of generating the good new ideas that businesses are looking for, especially in this AI world. What we're lacking is practice, courage and, as always, confidence. People who deliver good ideas have the same doubts about their creativity that we do, but they approach things differently.

Prof. Paul Torrance of the University of Georgia has conducted a 30-year follow-up study of highly successful creative people (whom he called the beyonders)[37] and found that these characteristics are common to all of them:

- delight in deep thinking,
- tolerance of mistakes,
- love of one's work,
- clear purpose,
- feeling comfortable as a minority of one,
- being different,
- not being well-rounded,
- sense of mission, and
- the courage to be creative.

IQ and academic achievements were not significant characteristics among the highly successful creative people.

In his book, *Originals: How Non-Conformists Move the World,*[38] psychologist Adam Grant explains that the creative process usually works as follows:

1. This is awesome.
2. This is tricky.
3. This is crap.
4. I am crap.
5. (This might be okay.
6. This is awesome.)

The problem, Grant says, is that self-doubt too often paralyses people at step four and they stop right there. The key is to shift from self-doubt to ideas-doubt and to avoid the leap from step three to step four. Instead of saying 'I'm crap', you say 'the first few drafts are always crap, and I'm just not there yet.' The famous author Ernest Hemingway is quoted as saying: 'The first draft of anything is shit.' The greatest originals are those who fail the most. It's important to keep trying – the greater your output, the greater your chances of success.

INSTEAD OF SAYING 'I'M CRAP', YOU SAY 'THE FIRST FEW DRAFTS ARE ALWAYS CRAP, AND I'M JUST NOT THERE YET.'

Other tips are to give yourself plenty of time – let your ideas sit, file your first draft and only go back to it after a few days. **Question your work, not yourself**. And, like everything else, the more you practise, the better you get. Collaborate with others, preferably people from backgrounds that are different to yours. If it's a work problem, bring in new ideas from different industries to help you challenge your thinking. Ask yourself what Elon Musk would suggest.

There's research[39] that shows that walking opens up the free flow of ideas, and it is a simple and robust solution to the goal of increasing creativity. So, when you are facing a sticky problem at work, go outside for a walk and you may well find, when you are back at your desk, that the ideas on how to move forward are suddenly right in front of you.

De Brabandere and Schwartz from the Boston Consulting Group suggest there are five essential steps to generating the big creative business ideas[40]:

1. **Doubt everything** – put on new lenses to look at the world, challenge your current perspective.
2. **Probe the possible** – explore what the world could look like.

3. **Diverge** – generate as many ideas as possible, even crazy ones.
4. **Converge** – evaluate which ideas will work.
5. **Re-evaluate constantly** – no idea is a good idea forever.

It will work well in a company brainstorm and your bosses will probably love it.

No idea is a good idea forever. The world changes too fast for that. The positive psychologists say that the answer to being creative lies in being open to new experiences, having a willingness to take risks, and having the motivation to keep trying. You just need to be confident that you do have awesome ideas.

> 'You can't use up creativity. The more you use, the more you have.'
>
> **MAYA ANGELOU**

4.13 Growing a thick skin

> 'Learn how to take criticism seriously but not personally.' **HILARY CLINTON**

Criticism can kill your confidence, especially if it is ongoing. Here are some ideas on how to handle criticism so that it doesn't crush you:

- Accept that criticism is inevitable and know that there are ways to handle it. First of all, assess where the criticism came from. For example, ignore criticism from trolls and idiots on social media and from clients who aren't paying their bills. Don't bother about criticism from anyone you wouldn't accept advice from.
- If it is from someone you don't rate, then treat what they think of you as their problem, not yours, and, in your mind, screw their criticism into a ball and chuck it in the wastepaper basket. Don't give people power over you.
- If the criticism is from someone you do rate, then it's worth taking the time to think about what has been said or written. Is there some truth in it? Can you learn from what happened? Our critics can be our best teachers.

If you don't think the criticism is fair, then don't go into battle; rather have a discussion where you look for common ground and try to understand the other person's intention.

What can you do if you are working for a boss who constantly criticises and undermines you? These are some coping mechanisms:Remember, it's not necessarily about you. Often the boss is insecure about their role or ability and takes it out on someone they think will be weak.

- Learn what to ignore. Choose to take criticism in your stride rather than let it get to you. Try to grow a thick skin the way call centre client service people who handle complaints and insults all day must.
- Reach out to your colleagues or a mentor for support.
- Don't argue directly with your boss because he or she is unlikely to back down. Confrontation rarely works. Rather listen, acknowledge and go back and do your work to the best of your ability. Try to let it slide.
- Maintain your integrity. Deliver your work on time as promised. Show that you are capable.
- If all else fails, ask for a transfer or look for a new job if that is feasible. You deserve better.

> LET'S BE THE PERSON WHO INSPIRES OTHERS, WHO DOESN'T LOOK FOR SCAPEGOATS BUT FOCUSES ON FIXING THE PROBLEM AND DEVELOPING THE TEAM.

Think again about the negativity bias covered in 2.8. Your brain is genetically programmed to dwell on negative inputs – so it's up to you to consciously choose to discard useless criticism and get on with your life!

Let's be the person who inspires others, who doesn't look for scapegoats but focuses on fixing the problem and developing the team. Find ways to build people up rather than tear them down. The famous activist, Charlotte Maxeke, told us: 'If you can rise, bring someone with you.'

If you must hold someone accountable, focus on the facts and not on opinions. Be gentle; we all know what it is like to be on the receiving end of criticism.

> 'I pay no attention whatever to anybody's praise or blame. I simply follow my own feelings.'
>
> **WOLFGANG AMADEUS MOZART**

4.14 Growth mindset

> 'A failure is not a mistake; it may simply be the best one can do in the circumstances. The real mistake is to stop trying.' **B. F. SKINNER**

Have you ever thought about how you look at the world? There are glass-half-full and glass-half-empty people, but there are also two different ways we think about challenges and setbacks, and about our own talents and abilities.

Based on extensive research, Professor Carol Dweck[41] of Stanford University argues that there are two different mindsets or ways of viewing the world. The two mindsets – a fixed mindset and a growth mindset – will affect everything: how confident you will be and even how successful you will be. Your way of thinking, your mindset, affects what you want and whether you will achieve it.

People who believe they have a certain intelligence and a fixed set of skills and are a certain type of personality have what is called a fixed mindset. With this mindset, people believe

> YOUR WAY OF THINKING, YOUR MINDSET, AFFECTS WHAT YOU WANT AND WHETHER YOU WILL ACHIEVE IT.

their ability is something they are born with and it's not possible to change it. People are either sporty, intelligent, artistic, good at maths, kind, disorganised or they're not. If people believe this, then they will tend to look at the world to confirm their view. Because their confidence is fragile and must be protected, fixed mindset folk will, according to Dweck, evaluate every situation in terms of 'Will they succeed or fail?' 'Will they look smart or dumb?' 'Will they be accepted or rejected?' 'Will they feel like a winner or a loser?' They will try to avoid failure, mistakes and criticism because they believe that it is riskier to try and fail than not try at all – they are the ones who never put up their hand. Fixed mindset believers think that if they have to struggle and work hard, it proves that they are 'not a natural'.

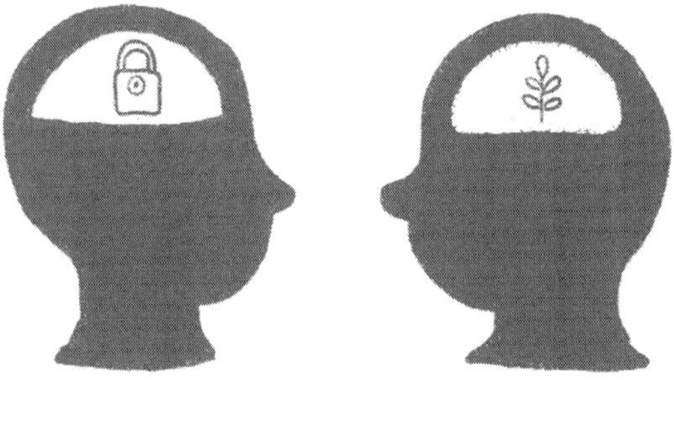

People who have a growth mindset believe that they can improve through effort and hard work. They believe that they can cultivate their basic qualities through experiences that stretch them. It is a fact that all people have huge potential for growth and development because, throughout our lives, our brains can form new neural pathways. You may have heard the term neuroplasticity or brain plasticity, which is the ability of the brain to modify its connections or rewire itself. Without this ability, the brain would be unable to develop from infancy through to adulthood or recover from brain injury.

So, once we accept that we can get good at things we thought we couldn't do at all, once we believe that tackling new experiences will make us grow personally or professionally, we can worry less about appearing smart or talented and put our energy into learning. Carol Dweck says: 'The passion for stretching yourself and sticking to it, even (or especially) when it's not going well, is the hallmark of the growth mindset. This is the mindset that allows people to thrive during some of the most challenging times in their lives.'

South African writer and thought leader Paballo Chauke writes: 'Whether you like it or not, you are going to fail, in different areas of your life, many times. Refuse to make failing or the fear thereof your identity. Even after failing, refuse to wear failure. Acknowledge that you failed, crumble if you need to, share your experience with others, but you have to dust yourself off. Refuse to be associated with failure – even though there are lessons in failing, we are not meant to stay there.'

Nosipho Dumisa, the 32-year-old director behind the hit South African Netflix series *Blood & Water*, said: 'Over the past 11 years there have been a lot of difficulties along the way. It was a very difficult process, but everything was leading to the next thing. And there were a lot of disappointments. But for me, I look at the disappointments as part of the journey towards getting to where we wanted to go.' Just days after that interview in a national newspaper, Netflix announced that *Blood & Water* had been given the go-ahead for a second season.

10 suggestions for developing a growth mindset

- ☺ Believe in yourself and your abilities.
- ☺ Know that you have the capacity to change and grow.
- ☺ Reframe failure differently. Ask 'what can I learn from this?'
- ☺ Accept that improvement is not the same as failure. Room for improvement is just space for more learning.
- ☺ Accept and welcome challenges.
- ☺ Be tenacious; keep trying.
- ☺ Always be curious.
- ☺ Value the process of learning as much as what you achieve.
- ☺ Recognise that talent is not enough; to succeed, you also need hard work.
- ☺ Capitalise on your strengths.

> 'It's not that I'm so smart, it's just that I stay with problems longer.'
>
> **ALBERT EINSTEIN**

4.15 Resilience

> 'Do not judge me by my success; judge me by how many times I fell down and got back up again.'
>
> **NELSON MANDELA**

Resilience is the ability to bounce back when you hit challenges, difficulties and setbacks. It's a very important skill in building confidence because the way you cope with negative experiences gives you the self-belief to keep moving forward rather than collapsing in a heap.

COVID-19 challenged everyone's resilience and many people were hit very hard because of the deaths of loved ones, losing their jobs and even being exposed to domestic violence. Yet others managed to do okay – adapting, enduring and continuing to function relatively normally.

What makes some people more resilient than others? Resilience is partly a result of our genes, partly a function of how we were brought up and partly due to the culture we were raised in. Your genes will play a part in determining how your body reacts to stress, but there are a lot of other factors that help build resilience, including:

- **Self-awareness**. Being aware of your thoughts and emotions (see 2.7), and being able to manage your reactions, for example through breathing (see 3.6).and being mindful (see 2.12).
- **Self-regulation**. Being able to change your thoughts by focusing on other things. Having goals and working towards them (see 4.8).
- **Mental agility**. Seeing things from different perspectives, being flexible (see 5.5).
- **Optimism**: Having a belief in a positive future. Having a growth mindset (see 4.14), which can see stressors as challenges, not threats. Sorting out what you can change and what you can't.
- **Self-efficacy**. Knowing your strengths and recognising your talents (see 3.8).
- **Connection**. Having people you can rely on, good relationships. For many, it's a feeling of being connected to something bigger than yourself, in the spiritual sense or though having a personal mission (see 5.1).
- **Positive institutions**. Being in a supportive family, community or workplace.

Resilient people understand that shit happens but they choose to focus on what they can change. **They know that failure is temporary but giving up is permanent.** I really admire the people who, when their livelihoods collapsed as a result of Covid, faced the challenges head on. I have a lot of friends in tourism and their income dried up overnight – some started sourcing goods and selling them online, others started teaching English to foreign students, others began baking to order, others started assisting home-schoolers with schoolwork. All these amazing people focused on what they could do and what they could control, rather than on what they had lost. Many have ended up with new careers as a result.

A note of caution, however: refusal to give up on a plan that is consistently failing is not an act of resilience. It's being rigid and it doesn't help to persevere with something that isn't working. Rather focus on your goal but be flexible about how you get there.

RESILIENT PEOPLE UNDERSTAND THAT SHIT HAPPENS BUT THEY CHOOSE TO FOCUS ON WHAT THEY CAN CHANGE.

What are the characteristics of resilient employees?

- They speak up, ask questions, are curious.
- They share bad news and potential problems and don't hide them.
- They look for expertise when they need help.
- They don't find disagreements risky.
- They put energy into what they are doing.
- They persevere.
- They listen well and communicate well.
- They can change direction if that's what is needed.

Whenever I'm facing upheavals, I like to remember the saying: 'Tough times don't last but tough people do.'

'THE WAY YOU COPE WITH NEGATIVE EXPERIENCES CAN GIVE YOU THE SELF-BELIEF TO KEEP MOVING FORWARD.'

'The most important thing I've learned when facing bleak circumstances is to choose hope over despair. Sometimes our problems seem as if they will never end. But as one of my favourite Buddhist sayings goes, 'Winter always turns to spring.' My challenges can either make me a better version of myself or break me apart, and I have a choice as to which it will be. It's so important to remember that you do have a choice, even when it feels as if you don't. I choose to be hopeful and to honour each experience in my life, negative and positive, as a chance to increase my wisdom, courage, and compassion.' **TINA TURNER**

4.16 The magic of mentors

> 'A mentor is someone who allows you to see the hope inside yourself.'
>
> **OPRAH WINFREY**

A mentor can be a big help. No matter what point you are at in your life, having a sounding board is invaluable. A mentor is an experienced and trusted advisor who can give you guidance and support and work with you to build your confidence.

Here's how mentors can help:

- By guiding you to clearly define your goals and what your next move should be.
- By giving you constructive feedback, both positive and negative, and even a reality check if that's what's needed.
- By identifying your strengths as well as possible gaps in your knowledge or skills.
- By giving you practical advice and useful insights.
- By expanding your view of the world, giving you a broader perspective.
- By encouraging you.

- By inspiring you.
- By sharing their experience and mistakes so that you don't need to make the same ones. (After all, your mentor has been there, done that, has the T-shirt.)
- By holding you accountable. If you make a commitment to your mentor, they will expect you to be true to your word (integrity in 2.2) and you're more likely to follow through on your promises.
- By giving you access to a wider network. Perhaps your mentor can introduce you to people that will be helpful in your career or introduce you to an expert who can solve the specific problem you're struggling with. They know people who know people.

So where do you find this magical mentor? Some companies run formal mentoring programmes that you can enrol in, but otherwise you need to start by working out what you want from your mentor. If you want advice on specific challenges, you need to identify someone who is an expert in your field. If you're looking for support and more general guidance, then select someone who is recognised for their people skills and wisdom. You shouldn't choose your direct boss as a mentor because it is hard for them to be objective. Don't be scared to approach someone to be your mentor – you'll be surprised how willing people are to help. Some people welcome the chance to develop mentoring skills as part of their own development, others just want to give back.

Any mentor you choose should be someone you respect and with whom you can build trust. Choose someone you admire, whose talent and achievements you look up to. Look for a person who is far enough from your situation to be unbiased.

Once you have identified a mentor and you've mutually agreed to the mentoring programme, you need to take responsibility for making the relationship work. Be respectful of your mentor's time, arrange a meeting schedule, honour your commitments, be flexible and acknowledge their help.

> 'Mentoring is a brain to pick, an ear to listen, and a push in the right direction.' **JOHN CROSBY**

4.17 Ten confidence no-nos

The behaviours in the box below are among the top killers of confidence. Do any of them ring a bell? If you're guilty of some of these, try taking one at a time and commit to working on changing that behaviour over the next month. Then pick another.

- Holding back.
- People pleasing.
- Lounging around in your comfort zone.
- Not taking a decision.
- Obsessing about your appearance.
- Pointless perfection.
- Catastrophising.
- Not taking responsibility.
- Not owning your successes.
- Avoiding any confrontation.

4.18 Khuthala's story

> 'I dug deep and kept reminding myself of who I was, and that what I knew was valuable.'

Khuthala Gala's fabulous smile and vivacious laughter instantly puts everyone at ease. There's no big ego here, yet when you start talking about brand marketing and advertising, you know immediately that you're talking to a real pro. Small wonder that before she was 40, Khuthala was already Managing Director of Joe Public United, South Africa's most awarded ad agency.

Khuthala was born in Langa, Cape Town, and was fostered by a white mom when she was young. Her foster mom, Glyn, was a single mother, fiercely independent, and a very successful entrepreneur, founding Delaney's promotions agency that had corporate clients like Woolworths and SFW. After matriculating, Khuthala joined Glyn, taking responsibility for running live events in bars and taverns although still in her teens. When ill health and some bad decisions forced her foster mom to close her business, Khuthala worked for a start-up agency in Cape Town, running branded

KHUTHALA'S INHERENT CREATIVE ABILITY AND BEING ABLE TO TALK TO ALL SEGMENTS OF THE TARGET MARKET SAW HER CAREER TAKE OFF.

promotions for huge corporates like Distell. *Was she scared? Was confidence a problem?* 'No,' says Khuthala. 'I was young and I wasn't scared of anything. I was passionate about what I was doing. My clients were all older white males who accepted that I knew about both the youth market and the black market.' Khuthala's inherent creative ability and being able to talk to all segments of the target market saw her career take off.

She was headhunted to work in Johannesburg by a more traditional ad agency. She was the Client Director at Unilever, the ultimate hierarchical corporate. *Was she nervous? Was confidence an issue then?* 'All my clients at Unilever had fancy degrees, and yet often they couldn't take a simple decision. It was easy to start doubting myself, but I dug deep and kept reminding myself of who I was, and that what I knew was valuable. I was determined to learn as much as possible, to soak up information like a sponge. When people are insecure they often just talk to impress, but I was happy to listen in meetings and make my contribution afterwards, back at the agency. I think humility is important.'

Headhunted again by Joe Public, Khuthala jumped at the opportunity to become a leader. She could see a huge opportunity. 'When you succeed, your motivation just grows; it's like a fuel. I was determined to succeed – so many people depended on me. No matter the obstacles, no matter the personal tragedies back home, I had to find a way to deliver.' *Is confidence an issue in her MD role?* 'Sometimes I feel a bit of imposter syndrome creeping in – here I am, sitting around the boardroom table with these top, top business people and I don't have a tertiary education. I ask myself: "Am I just window dressing?" But then I think about my skill set – I'm experienced, well travelled, articulate – and I tell myself I am the best man you could ever put in your window! And those butterflies are good – the adrenalin makes you perform better.'

I ask Khuthala about her team. *Is confidence an issue with her younger staff members?* 'Yes,' she says, 'and it's often cultural. Black women are brought up to be polite to their elders, so they struggle to challenge older clients or colleagues.

Our history and upbringing means that they have a different energy with white clients than with black clients. In a new job, they are too nervous or shy to ask if they didn't understand something and so they can make mistakes, and that undermines their confidence even more.' *How does she build confidence with her team then?* 'I point out that a lot of our anxiety is based on things that aren't there or aren't going to happen. Also, if there is a problem, I don't believe in blame games – I'd rather fix the problem. No one comes to work determined to make a mistake. I don't sweat the small stuff. I'm sensitive to the fact that often first jobs are so challenging – people don't yet have their own cars, they might live far away and need to take taxis, plus they have the pressure of family obligations and they may not yet have the resilience to balance it all.'

Joe Public United had these themes highlighted on their website: Creativity, excellence, integrity, respect, leadership and unity. Khuthala certainly embodies them.

Here is Khuthala's favourite quote:

> 'Failure is an important part of your growth and developing resilience. Don't be afraid to fail.' **MICHELLE OBAMA**

5.
Building your future

5.1 Do you have a why?

> 'For there is always light
> if we are brave enough to see it
> if we are brave enough to be it.'
>
> **AMANDA GORMAN**

At training workshops and motivational seminars, the course leader often asks the attendees to think about their own funeral and what they think people at the service will say about them. What is it you would like to be remembered for? Thinking about this is a way for you to work out what is important to you. It's humbling to think that you're more likely to be remembered for loving your family or helping the community than for being the MD of a company or making lots of money.

The founder of Positive Psychology, Professor Martin Seligman, believes that the antidote to depression is for people to live more meaningful lives, and that meaning is about serving a purpose higher than yourself. It can be about having the *ikigai* that is described in 5.2 or supporting charities or selflessly helping your family. He says that the best way to do this is to work with your individual strengths (see 3.7) because it is easier to get involved with activities that interest you and where you can add the most value.

This search for meaning is often described as **finding your Why**. Some coaches call it having a vision. It's more than just a goal for your career; it's how you want to think about your whole life and how you live it. We look for our purpose and our significance so that we can understand our lives better and make sense of the world. And everyone will have a different Why.

If you are struggling to find meaning, making connections and building relationships with people who make you feel that you belong will give your life more purpose. So, put energy into your friends, old and new, and into your family. Get involved with your community. And finding a hobby or interest that makes you happy will also bring more meaning into your life – it could be reading or hiking or painting or taking up tennis or learning a new language – and you can use your hobby to link up with like-minded people. Finding a passion that is yours and developing it will give you something to talk about. I love what South African ad agency director Mpume Ngobese told me: 'Finding and owning your passion and knowing you are a guru on something will build your confidence because you won't be living your life floating around, questioning who you are. You are your own unique path.'

Simone de Beauvoir was a French philosopher, writer and women's activist in the last century and this is what she wrote about life's meaning: 'Growing, ripening, ageing, dying – the passing of time is predestined, inevitable. There is only one solution if old age is not to be an absurd parody of our former life, and that is to go on pursuing ends that give our existence a meaning – devotion to individuals, to groups or to causes, social, political, intellectual or creative work … In old age we should wish still to have passions strong enough to prevent us turning in on ourselves. One's life has value so long as one attributes value to the life of others, by means of love, friendship, indignation, compassion.'

Ruth Bader Ginsberg was a judge of the American Supreme Court, and throughout her life she fought for justice and equality for women and for civil rights. She battled two bouts of cancer and continued her work as a judge up until her death in 2020 at the age of 87. Here's what she wrote about meaning: 'If you want to be a true professional, you will do something outside yourself. Something to repair tears in your community. Something to make life a little better for people less fortunate than you. That's what I think a meaningful life is – living not for oneself, but for one's community.'

Don't just be a visitor to this life; add value to it.

> 'He who has a why can endure any how.' **FRIEDRICH NIETZSCHE**

5.2 *Ikigai*

> 'Everyone has been made for some particular work and the desire for that work has been put in every heart.' **RUMI**

Imagine if it weren't the alarm going off that got you out of bed every morning. What if it were a sense of purpose? A feeling of joy? Living your Why, your vision for yourself.

The Japanese have a word for your reason for being – ikigai. Ikigai comes from two Japanese words, iki meaning life, and gai meaning value or worth. In a seven-year longitudinal study of 43,000 Japanese adults, researchers at Tohoku University in Sendai[42] found that people who believed that their lives had ikigai lived significantly longer than those claiming not to have ikigai. A more recent study published in 2022[43] showed that people with ikigai had a lower incidence of depression, a 36% lower risk of developing dementia, and had more happiness and life satisfaction.

Ikigai is more than just vaguely following your passion or your dreams; it should challenge you and involve a serious commitment to your vision.

It can be about family, people, the greater good, mastering a hobby, or success in your career. For example, being a bus conductor is not having *ikigai*, but if you are determined to be the very best and friendliest bus conductor ever, who makes sure everyone on the bus has a safe and pleasant ride, then you will have found your *ikigai*.

To find your *ikigai*, start with three lists. The first one should be your values, the second one your strengths, and the third one what you are good at. (Check out 3.7 on Strengths.) Look at where your lists intersect, and then add the question: 'What can I get paid for?' because we all have to earn a living.

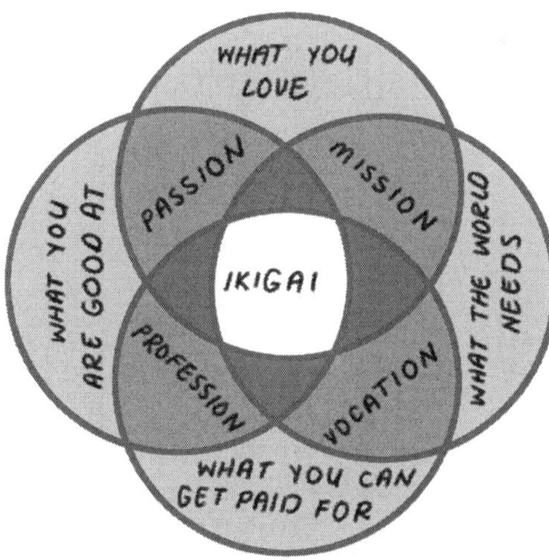

Diagram first drawn by Marc Winn

THE CONFIDENCE THAT COMES FROM KNOWING WHO YOU ARE AND WHAT YOU WANT TO DO WITH YOUR LIFE IS A SUPERPOWER.

When you can link what you are 'good at' with your personal passion, you will be connecting to who you fundamentally are, the authentic you. The confidence that comes from knowing who you are and what you want to do with your life is another superpower.

> 'I've come to believe that each of us has a personal calling that's as unique as a fingerprint – and that the best way to succeed is to discover what you love and then find a way to offer it to others in the form of service, working hard, and also allowing the energy of the universe to lead you.' **OPRAH WINFREY**

5.3 Getting your grit on with *sisu*

> 'It always seems impossible until it's done.' **NELSON MANDELA**

Saray Khumalo was the first black African woman to summit Everest. Did you know that before her success, she had had three failed attempts? In 2014, she was stopped after an avalanche killed 16 guides. The following year she was halted by the earthquake that ravaged Nepal, and on her third attempt in 2017, atrocious weather forced the climbers to turn back. Three near-death experiences? I would have decided that the mountain was telling me to stop and go home for good. But Saray never gave up on her dream, and in May 2019 she conquered Everest to stand among the stars.

Thinking about never giving up leads us to *sisu*. *Sisu* is a Finnish concept that doesn't translate into a single word – it's a combination of grit, courage, perseverance and the determination to keep going against the odds. The Finns believe that it is a national characteristic that defined them as a nation when, in the Winter War of 1939 to 1940, the tiny nation withstood the invasion by Russia and retained their independence. Saray Khumalo has *sisu* in bucket loads.

We can tap into our *sisu* when we take a consistent, courageous approach to challenges that seem beyond our capabilities. When we run into really difficult situations, we can choose to look for the opportunities to win through. *Sisu* is a reserve of power that enables extraordinary action from ordinary people and, like all our abilities, the more we practise it, the more we develop it. We have all seen it in people who have had awful accidents and learn to walk or talk again when science has said it would never be possible.

It's *sisu* that enables a woman in her 50s, from a disadvantaged background, to graduate with a doctorate. It's *sisu* that keeps you at it until you finally achieve the Maths grade that you need to get into the course you want to study. It's *sisu* when you complete the marathon despite your cramping legs. It's *sisu* that keeps you building your own small business when it seems everything is stacked against you.

The famous South African endurance swimmer Lewis Pugh was the first person to complete a long-distance swim in all five oceans of the world, including a swim in open sea with a temperature of minus 1.7°C across the North Pole. He has swum across Lake Pumori, a glacial lake on Mount Everest, to highlight the melting of the glaciers in the Himalayas. Lewis swims in a Speedo! Here's his advice on true grit: 'The temptation to quit will be strongest shortly after you've begun, and just before you finish. If you're aware of it, you can avoid it. The reason is simple: At the start, it can be overwhelming and much harder than you expected. Likewise, when you're near the end, you're exhausted and need utter determination to finish.'

NEXT TIME YOU FEEL YOU HAVE REACHED THE END OF THE ROAD, AND EVERYONE IS TELLING YOU IT IS ENOUGH, THEN THINK SISU ...

You can be inspired by thinking about examples of people doing seemingly impossible things and by thinking about the times you yourself have managed what you once thought was impossible. Next time you feel you have reached the end of the road, and everyone is telling you it is enough, then think *sisu*, dig deep for your fighting spirit and don't give up.

> 'Grit is living life like it's a marathon, not a sprint.' **ANGELA DUCKWORTH**

5.4 Wave goodbye to your comfort zone

> 'One can choose to go back toward safety or forward toward growth. Growth must be chosen again and again; fear must be overcome again and again.' **ABRAHAM MASLOW**

Being comfortable can be good. Certainly, being comfortably off is good. Settling down for some me-time on a comfy sofa is good. But being stuck in your comfort zone for any length of time isn't good. Why? Because it means you can't grow. You're like that lemon tree in your garden that doesn't die but never gets any bigger and never flowers or fruits.

What is a comfort zone?

The phrase 'comfort zone' was coined by management thinker Judith Bardwick in her 1991 book Danger in the Comfort Zone. She defined it like this: 'The comfort zone is a behavioural state within which a person operates in an anxiety-neutral condition, using a limited set of behaviours to deliver a steady level of performance, usually without a sense of risk.'

> BUT DEEP DOWN WE KNOW THERE IS MORE INSIDE OF US AND ALL WE NEED IS THE CONFIDENCE TO STEP INTO A MORE EXCITING VERSION OF OURSELVES.

Our comfort zone is an easy space to live in because we feel in control and we feel safe. Many of us stick in dead-end jobs because we like the secure feeling that comes with doing the same thing day after day. But deep down we know there is more inside of us and all we need is the confidence to step into a more exciting version of ourselves.

The reason many folk don't grow is that they are fearful. 'I couldn't do that job.' 'What if I fail?' 'I've got no experience in that field.' They worry about what other people will think and so they find excuses like 'I'm not ready yet' 'I've got a young family' 'I need to study first' 'Maybe next year.'

There are comfort zones in any part of your life – career, relationships, friendships, habits, hobbies, even your sport. In relationships, people may remain with unsatisfactory, or even destructive partners because they are too fearful about being on their own and scared they will never find someone else.

One way of facing up to the fear of change is to take small steps and make small lifestyle changes. Read a book by an author you don't know, try a different recipe, switch to another brand, get up at a different time, walk a different route. Then move on to bigger changes like visiting a different part of the country, redecorating, acquiring a new hobby, learning another language or meeting new people. When we feel successful making tiny changes, the next steps are so much easier.

Be inspired by this quote from the musician Ronnie Oldham: 'Excellence is the result of caring more than others think is wise, risking more than others think is safe, dreaming more than others think is practical, and expecting more than others think is possible.'

When you see you that you can change, it changes the way you see yourself. It's only in the growth zone that you will get new skills, deal with challenges and start making dreams come true. As you start to succeed, your belief in yourself will grow and so will your dreams.

> 'Do one thing every day that scares you.' **ELEANOR ROOSEVELT**

5.5 Lifelong learning

> 'Questions you cannot answer are better for you than answers you cannot question.' **YUVAL NOAH HARARI**

In 1960, when the United Nations first began keeping records, the global average life expectancy was 52.5 years. Today it is 72. And in many countries the projections suggest that most people alive today will live well into their 90s and beyond. That's a long time after most people have retired. Not only that, if the past 20 years are anything to go by, think how much will change in that time. As the historian Yuval Harari writes: 'Given that life expectancy is likely to increase, you might have to spend many decades as a clueless fossil.'[44]

I don't want to become a clueless fossil, so I do my best to carry on reading and learning, even though the pace of change sometimes make me feel dizzy. I know that among the issues we will face are climate change disasters, water wars, new pandemics, ethics around gene editing, increasingly polarised and unequal societies, AI, computers that think, and probably people living on Mars – but what else will there be?

These are just some of the big changes of the past 20 years – not in any order.

Smartphones
Streaming videos (Netflix 2007)
3D printing
Vaping
Blockchain
Bitcoin
Non-fungible tokens
eReaders
Podcasts
Electric self-drive cars
Gene editing
Tapping credit cards
Siri, Alexa
Twitter/X, Instagram, TikTok
Augmented reality
Esports (electronic sports)
COVID-19
Drones
Artificial intelligence (AI)
ChatGPT
Web3

The world is changing fast and so if you're not changing with it, then you're getting left behind. If you want to protect yourself and benefit from change, you need to be able to look around the corner and ask: 'What is unthinkable today but could be common a few years from now?'

Ask yourself

- ☺ What's my biggest work-related fear?
- ☺ What careers would I suggest to young people in high school?
- ☺ Will my career still exist in 10 years' time?
- ☺ What am I doing to stay relevant?
- ☺ What new skill did I acquire this year?
- ☺ What new skill will I acquire next year?

We will have to constantly learn new stuff, adapt, accept new challenges and embrace new ways of living. Robots or artificial intelligence may take over the jobs we once had; jobs like travel agent, cashier and bank teller are already becoming obsolete. If we want to keep earning an income, we will probably have to reinvent ourselves and even change careers a few times. This pace of change with its growing uncertainty is going to add massively to most people's stress levels. Being made redundant at work can totally undermine your belief in yourself and your confidence in the future, so take steps to future-proof yourself as much as possible.

We are incredibly lucky in that our brains can keep learning – our brains are phenomenal. Earlier (4.14) I mentioned 'neuroplasticity' – the ability of the brain to modify its connections or rewire itself. The brain continues to change with learning and experience throughout our lives so we are able to learn new things even into our old age.

A new future is going to be here tomorrow. What can we do?

- ☺ Leave our comfort zone.
- ☺ Embrace lifelong learning.
- ☺ Always be curious. Find out more, ask questions.
- ☺ Look at problems from as many points of view as possible.
- ☺ Accept uncertainty, tolerate ambiguity.
- ☺ Develop good communication skills.
- ☺ Keep studying. Take short courses through online learning – they aren't expensive.
- ☺ Don't be afraid to try new stuff – when a child learns to walk, she falls over all the time.

BEING MADE REDUNDANT AT WORK CAN TOTALLY UNDERMINE YOUR BELIEF IN YOURSELF AND YOUR CONFIDENCE IN THE FUTURE, SO TAKE STEPS TO FUTURE-PROOF YOURSELF AS MUCH AS POSSIBLE.

Learning keeps your brain alive. **You're never too old.** The story goes that a TV anchor once asked Grand Slam tennis champion Martina Navratilova: 'How do you maintain your focus and manage to keep playing, even at the age of 43?' Her simple answer was: 'The ball doesn't know how old I am.'

> 'I've learned that I still have a lot to learn.' **MAYA ANGELOU**

5.6 The meaning of money

> 'You must gain control over your money or the lack of it will forever control you.' **DAVE RAMSEY**

Finance isn't my area of interest, but I can't write about confidence without mentioning money, because money enables confidence.

I'm not talking about money for insanely expensive watches and super fast cars and similar ego items. That kind of wealth isn't achievable for most of us. I'm talking about the money that means you can make a choice. The money that brings the ability to leave a toxic relationship and put down the deposit to rent your own place. Enough money to leave a bad job and survive while you look for another. The money to replace a smashed phone or a stolen laptop. That's financial confidence.

If you are earning well, you do feel proud and more confident. If you are struggling to afford rent and food and other essentials, you can feel incompetent and hopeless. If this happens to you, acknowledge your feelings, be determined not to give up, and try to focus on what you can do to change your situation.

Once you are making good money, start thinking about what is enough. Some people are endlessly driven to make more and more money, but often it doesn't make them happy. We are conditioned to equate money with success and to see possessions as proof of our status. But, once you can uncouple your confidence from money, you can identify what is enough for you (and that is different for everyone) and experience the freedom to enjoy your life without being chained to the treadmill.

Confident people never ignore money basics because they think finance is too complicated or loathed accounting at school. We all need to have a budget, understand compound interest and make the wisest possible financial decisions.

IF YOU ARE EARNING WELL, YOU DO FEEL PROUD AND MORE CONFIDENT. IF YOU ARE STRUGGLING TO AFFORD RENT AND FOOD AND OTHER ESSENTIALS, YOU CAN FEEL INCOMPETENT AND HOPELESS.

Here are 10 things you should do from your very first paycheque:

1. Draw up a budget that balances your income and expenses. Banking phone apps can help you with this.
2. Check mid-month that you're staying within your budget.
3. Take 15% of what you are earning and put it into savings. Stick with this 15% even when you are earning more – especially when you are earning more!
4. Begin saving by building up an emergency fund that you can access quickly in an emergency.
5. Then, as soon as you can, start saving for your retirement. With compound interest, even small amounts grow into substantial amounts over time. Retirement may seem ridiculously far away, but one day you will get there and data shows that 50% of American and 90% of South African retirees cannot maintain their standard of living once they retire.
6. Join a good medical scheme, even if it is only a hospital plan. And then buy top-up insurance – it's relatively cheap and a big help if you do land up in hospital.

7. Get life cover if you have dependants.
8. If you switch jobs, make sure you protect your pension.
9. Don't buy a brand-new car. New cars lose about 10% of their value as you drive away from the dealership. Look for a demo model or a relatively new second-hand one.
10. If someone offers you an incredible return on your investment, be careful. Research it thoroughly. If it sounds too good to be true, it usually is too good to be true.

> 'Money can buy you a fine dog, but only love can make him wag his tail.'
>
> **KINKY FRIEDMAN**

5.7 Top ten ways forward

> 'We delight in the beauty of the butterfly, but rarely admit the changes it has gone through to achieve that beauty.' **MAYA ANGELOU**

- Live deeply. Live your why. Life goes by so fast.
- Failures are stepping stones to improving.
- Build quick wins.
- Speak up when it matters.
- Getting it done is better than being perfect.
- When the numbers add up, believe them.
- Always be curious.
- Choose to get out of your comfort zone.
- Try something new every week.
- Change what you are doing to change where you are going.

> 'Love the life you live. Live the life you love.' **BOB MARLEY**

5.8 Janet's story

> 'Nothing is impossible if you put in the right effort.' **JANET**

Once you've met Janet Pillai, you don't forget her. 'I own who I am', she tells me. Janet is a powerful presence, smart, glamorous and radiating energy. She is the founder and CEO of MLT Corporation, a very successful enterprise owning several companies spanning car rental, tourism and car repairs. But Janet's first love wasn't business – it was art, drama, languages and literature – and her fist formal job was as a museum curator.

Janet remembers her early childhood in KwaZulu-Natal with great affection. The youngest of six children, she recalls big parties, family picnics, her mother's love of beautiful clothes and of cooking, the smells of guavas, avocados, pickles and spices. Everything came from the large garden. The family wasn't wealthy, but rich in ideas – her father studied all his life, robust debate was encouraged, and the children were into reading, theatre and art. From a young age, Janet buried herself in books and studying. She worked extremely hard to excel in her studies, passing with distinction, which gave her the confidence to tackle many different challenges.

Along with her academic achievements at school and university, Janet was always working part-time and running side hustles. At high school, she gave art classes at her home and began working part-time in her brother's law firm. At university, she worked in a bottle store and later as a graduate assistant tutor.

Janet was always studying so that she could make the most of her opportunities. Working at her brother's law firm, she learnt to type and file, became a Commissioner of Oaths, passed the Estate Agent's exam and qualified as an evaluator. Typical of Janet's approach to life was taking a Mindmap course so that she could remember people's names when introduced. Later in her career she added a diploma in Public Relations and an Honours degree. Knowing a lot about a wide range of things was key to her early success.

Janet's dream was always to be a museum curator. When she finished university, there was no job like that available. For a full year, looking for her dream job preoccupied her – creatively visualising herself in the role she wanted –

ALWAYS ONE TO GRAB OPPORTUNITIES, JANET PUT A GREAT DEAL OF EFFORT AND OVERTIME INTO HER JOB.

until she landed the position of Curator and Visiting Fellow of Contemporary and Indigenous Collections at the University of Fort Hare. Janet believes she landed the job in the face of strong competition because she was so widely read across so many subjects. Her knowledge, along with the admin skills learnt in the law office, gave her the confidence to thrive in this role despite her lack of curating experience.

Always one to grab opportunities, Janet put a great deal of effort and overtime into her job.

She studied the collections in depth and started cataloguing collections that had been packed away for ages. Her reputation grew and she was asked to catalogue all the artwork in the liberation archives, and then Nelson Mandela's art collection at Tuynhuys. As a result, Janet got the chance to study at the Smithsonian Institute. She says: 'Putting in the effort brought the opportunities.'

Janet moved on to take the role of Director of Arts, Culture and Heritage for the Western Cape with a large staff complement of people reporting to her. The work was exciting but, in the end, the politics proved too stressful. Janet took time out and went back home to think and plan her next career. Consulting paid the bills until she started MLT. She began by going online and quoting to supply whatever was being requested. She had no inventory, no warehouse and no tendering experience, but she made it all happen.

At the end of year one, she bought MLT's first two cars with trading profits. Twenty years later, she has grown MLT into a sizable corporation, survived lockdown, and built her own offices. Janet agrees that she has taken many risks and faced many setbacks, but the courage and confidence she has needed is now in her DNA.

JANET AGREES THAT SHE HAS TAKEN MANY RISKS AND FACED MANY SETBACKS, BUT THE COURAGE AND CONFIDENCE SHE HAS NEEDED IS NOW IN HER DNA.

Today she identifies future leaders in her businesses by their willingness to put in the work, to go the extra mile – just as she herself always has. Then she builds their confidence by giving them opportunities to act independently, showing her trust in them and giving them space to learn.

Janet's latest venture is 'Jetsetting with Janet', which began with her hosting a slot on a local radio station. It has grown into a YouTube channel and a podcast. This is the creative side of Janet coming to the fore, owning who she is and doing what she loves.

And Janet's favourite quote?

> 'I do not know anyone who has got to the top without hard work. That is the recipe. It will not always get you to the top, but should get you pretty near.' **MARGARET THATCHER**

5.9 It's your time to shine

> 'You have brains in your head.
> You have feet in your shoes.
> You can steer yourself any direction you choose.
> You're on your own and you know what you know.
> And YOU are the guy who'll decide where to go.' **DR. SEUSS**

Thank you for choosing this book.

Be strong.
Walk tall.
Choose honesty.
Show compassion.
Acknowledge your worth.
Smile often.
You've got this!

♡ Su

6. Notes

Why confidence counts

1. Vicki Contie, 'Gene Linked to Optimism and Self-Esteem', National Institutes of Health, https://www.nih.gov/news-events/nih-research-matters/gene-linked-optimism-self-esteem, accessed 30 January 2023.
2. Martin E. P. Seligman, 'Learned optimism', notes by J. Zimmerman, http://www2.cruzio.com/~zdino/psychology/seligman.optimism.htm, accessed 30 January 2023.
3. Khatera Sahibzada, 'How to resist the lure of overconfidence', 2 August 2019, *Scientific American*, https://blogs.scientificamerican.com/observations/how-to-resist-the-lure-of-overconfidence/, accessed 30 January 2023.

Building you

4. Benjamin Laker, 'What does the four-day week mean for the future of work?', 16 May 2022, MIT *Sloan Management Review*, https://sloanreview.mit.edu/article/what-does-the-four-day-workweek-mean-for-the-future-of-work/, accessed 30 January 2023.

5. Katty Kay, Claire Shipman, *The Confidence Code* (New York, Harper Collins, 2014) p. 131.
6. Katty Kay, Claire Shipman, *The Confidence Code*, p. 201.
7. Edith Eger, *The Choice* (Rider, 2018).
8. Kumar, A., Killingsworth, M. A., Gilovich, T., 'Waiting for Merlot: Anticipatory Consumption of Experiential and Material Purchases', 2014, *Psychological Science*, 25(10), https://doi.org/10.1177/0956797614546556, accessed 12 December 2022.
9. Vaish, A., Grossman, T., Woodward, A., 'Not all emotions are created equal: The negativity bias in social-emotional development', 2008, *Psychological Bulletin*, 134(3): 383–403, https://psycnet.apa.org/record/2008-04614-0027a, accessed 5 June 2021.
10. Scott, E., 'How to practise loving kindness meditation', 11 February 2020, https://www.verywellmind.com/how-to-practice-loving-kindness-meditation-3144786, accessed 18 February 2021.
11. Escalante, A., 'New Science: Why our brains spend 50% of the time mind-wandering', 28 Jan 2021, *Forbes*, https://www.forbes.com/sites/alisonescalante/2021/01/28/new-science-why-our-brains-spend-50-of-the-time-mind-wandering/?sh=74cf751f4854, accessed 9 January 2023.
12. Killingsworth, A., Gilbert, D., 'A wandering mind is an unhappy mind', Science 2010 Nov 12;330(6006):932. https://pubmed.ncbi.nlm.nih.gov/21071660/, accessed 9 January 2023.

13. Emmons, R. A., Crumpler, C. A., 'Gratitude as a Human Strength: Appraising the Evidence', 2000, *Journal of Social and Clinical Psychology*: Vol. 19, No. 1, pp. 56–69, https://www.researchgate.net/publication/277433477_Gratitude_as_a_Human_Strength_Appraising_the_Evidence, accessed 5 June 2020.
14. The Greater Good Science Center, UC Berkeley, 'The science of gratitude', May 2018, https://ggsc.berkeley.edu/images/uploads/GGSC-JTF_White_Paper-Gratitude-FINAL.pdf, accessed 30 May 2020.
15. Lin, C-C., 'Self-esteem mediates the relationship between dispositional gratitude and wellbeing. Personality and Individual Differences', 2015, https://www.sciencedirect.com/science/article/abs/pii/S0191886915003086?via%3Dihub, accessed 2 December 2020.
16. Koo, M., Algoe, S. B., Wilson, T. D., Gilbert, D. T., 'It's a wonderful life: Mentally subtracting positive events improves people's affective states, contrary to their affective forecasts', 2008, *Journal of Personality and Social Psychology*, 95, 1217–1224, https://www.ncbi.nlm.nih.gov/pmc/articles/PMC2746912/, accessed 12 May 2022.
17. Sturm, V., 'Walks boost emotional wellbeing', 21 September 2020, *Neuroscience News*, https://neurosciencenews.com/awe-walk-emotional-wellbeing-17063/, accessed 20 January 2023.

Building your social life

18. Calogero, R. M., Boroughs, M., Thompson, J. K., 'The Impact of Western Beauty Ideals on the Lives of Women: A Sociocultural Perspective', 2007, https://doi.org/10.1057/9780230596887_13, accessed 11 May 2020.
19. Epley, N., Schroeder, J., 'Mistakenly seeking solitude', 2007, *Journal of Experimental Psychology: General*, 143(5), 1980–1999, https://doi.org/10.1037/a0037323, accessed 6 July 2020.
20. Boothby, E.J., Cooney, G., Sandstrom, J.M., Clark, M. S., 'The Liking Gap in Conversations: Do People like us more Than We Think?', 2018, *Psychological Science* vol 29, issue 11, https://doi.org/10.1177/0956797618783714, accessed 7 July 2020.
21. Covey, Stephen R., *The 7 Habits of Highly Effective People: Powerful Lessons in Personal Change*, Special Edition (New York, Simon & Schuster, 2013).
22. Edgar H. Schein, *Humble Inquiry: The Gentle Art of Asking Instead of Telling* (Oakland US, Berrett-Koehler Publishers, 2013).
23. Roger Martin, 'Think Like a leader', https://www.youtube.com/watch?v=ODWfSnNEcfg.
24. Abrahams, M., 'How to make a compelling pitch', 14 August 2023, *Harvard Business Review*, https://hbr.org/2023/08/how-to-make-a-compelling-pitch.
25. Carney, D. R., Cuddy, A. J., Yap, A. J., 'Power posing: brief nonverbal displays affect neuroendocrine levels and risk tolerance', 2010, *Psychol Sci.* 2010 Oct;21(10):1363–8. https://pubmed.ncbi.nlm.nih.gov/20855902/.

26. Briñol, P., Petty, R., Wagner, B., Body posture effects on self-evaluation: A self-evaluation approach, 2009, *European Journal of Social Psychology* 39. 1053–1064. 10.1002/ejsp.607.

Building your career

27. https://woopmylife.org/, accessed 30 June 2021.
28. https://www.paulineroseclance.com, accessed 7 January 2022.
29. Valerie Young, *The Secret Thoughts of Successful Women: Why Capable People Suffer from Impostor Syndrome and How to Thrive in Spite of It*, (Crown/Random House 2011).
30. Meredith Fineman, *Brag Better: Master the Art of Fearless Self-Promotion* (Portfolio 2020).
31. Zippia, '20 Vital Smartphone Usage Statistics [2023]: Facts, Data, and Trends On Mobile Use In The U.S.', Apr. 3, 2023, Zippia.com, https://www.zippia.com/advice/smartphone-usage-statistics/.
32. Huberman, A., 'Teach & Learn Better With A "Neuroplasticity Super Protocol"', 29 October 2021, https://hubermanlab.com/teach-and-learn-better-with-a-neuroplasticity-super-protocol/.
33. American Psychological Association, 'Multitasking: Switching costs', 20 March 2006, https://www.apa.org/topics/research/multitasking, accessed 16 August 2023.
34. Robbins, M., *The Five Second Rule. Transform your Life, Work, and Confidence with Everyday Courage* (Savio Republic, 2017).
35. Covey, Stephen R., *The 7 Habits of Highly Effective People* (New York, Simon & Schuster, 2013).

36. Woods, A. B., 'Get excited: Reappraising Performance Anxiety as Excitement', *Journal of Experimental Psychology*, 2014, https://www.apa.org/pubs/journals/releases/xge-a0035325.pdf.
37. Torrance, E. P., The beyonders in a thirty year longitudinal study of creative achievement, 1993, *Roeper Review*, 15(3), 131–135, https://doi.org/10.1080/02783199309553486.
38. Grant, A., *Originals: How Non-Conformists Move the World* (Viking, 2016).
39. Opezzo, M., Schwartz, D., 'Give Your Ideas Some Legs: The Positive Effect of Walking on Creative Thinking', 2014, *Journal of Experimental Psychology Learning Memory and Cognition* 40(4).
40. De Brabandere, L., Iny, A., *Thinking in New Boxes* (New York, Random House, 2013), p. 28.
41. Dweck, C., *Mindset: The new Psychology of Success* (Random House Publishing Group, 2007).

Building your future

42. Tsuji, I., Sone, T., 'Association between Sense of life Worth Living (ikigai) and Mortality Risk', 2007, https://www.bureau.tohoku.ac.jp/kohyo/kokusai/07Mar7News-full.htm, accessed 21 July 2023.
43. Okuzono, S. S., Shiba, K., Kim, E. S., Shirai, K., Kondo, N., Fujiwara, T., Kondo, K., Lomas, T., Trudel-Fitzgerald, C., Kawachi, I., VanderWeele, T. J., 'Ikigai and subsequent health and wellbeing among Japanese older adults: Longitudinal outcome-wide analysis', Lancet Reg Health West Pac. 2022.
44. Harari, Y. N., *21 lessons for the 21st century* (Random House, 2018).

Su Birch studied psychology and sociology at university, and later went on to study for an MBA. Throughout her very successful career, ultimately as CEO of an international marketing company, Su's greatest joy has been developing her teams. She is a qualified life coach, focusing on building confidence among young executives.

Printed in Great Britain
by Amazon

57449632R00130